A Sinner in Jannah

Stories of Repentance, Hope and Mercy

TRANSCRIBED AND ADAPTED FROM
"A SINNER IN JANNAH:
STORIES OF REPENTANCE, HOPE AND MERCY"
BY
YAHYA IBRAHIM

Published by:

TERTIB PUBLISHING

Unit No. E-10, 5 Jln SS 15/4G, Subang Square,
47500 Subang Jaya, Selangor, Malaysia
+603-5612-2407 (office) / +6017-399-7411 (mobile)
info@tertib.press
www.tertib.press
@tertibpress (Facebook & Instagram)

Author	:	Yahya Ibrahim
Transcriber & Editor	:	Nadiah Aslam
Proofreader	:	Norashikin Azizan
		Arisha Mohd Affendy
Cover designer	:	Abdul Adzim Md Daim
Typesetter	:	Abdul Adzim Md Daim

A SINNER IN JANNAH: STORIES OF REPENTANCE, HOPE AND MERCY

First Edition: April 2023

Cataloguing-in-Publication Data

Perpustakaan Negara Malaysia

A catalogue record for this book is available from the National Library of Malaysia

ISBN 978-967-2844-26-6

Contents

Preface

Assalamualaikum dear brothers and sisters,

Always and forever, we begin with the praise of Allah (s.w.t.). We send our prayers of peace upon our Prophet Muḥammad (s.a.w.). We testify with full firmness and conviction that none is worthy of worship but Allah and that Muḥammad (s.a.w.) is His worshipping slave and final messenger.

I continue to remind myself and you dear readers of *ittaqullah* (fear of Allah). I pray that Allah (s.w.t.) allows us to build, and increase our love for Him, our fear and our hope in His mercy as well. I pray that Allah (s.w.t.) makes this book a medium of *raḥmah* (mercy) and of our commitment to the sunnah and the ideals of the Prophet (s.a.w.). Peace and blessings be upon our Nabi (s.a.w.) and all of those who preceded him in *khayr* (good).

I pray that Allah makes the Qur'an the measure of our hearts, the compass of our guidance and the map of our life. I pray that Allah allows us the honour of being in the rank and in the file of our Prophet (s.a.w.) and that we

are recognised by him (s.a.w.) on the Day of Judgement on account of the markings of our *wudu'* (ablution). I pray that Allah (s.w.t.) favours us with his *shafa'ah* (intercession), as well as the *shafa'ah* of the Prophet (s.a.w.) as he (s.a.w.) ascends to *Al-Maqam al-Maḥmud* (the praised station), that has been promised to him (s.a.w.) by Allah (s.w.t.).

In this book, we will discuss about *Jannah*, the different types and categories of sin, the psychology of redemption and *tawbah* (repentance), as well as the straight path—*al-Siraṭal-Mustaqim*.

Jannah should be our ultimate goal. It should be our goal to enter *Jannah*. *Jannah* is Allah's mercy towards us. How do we get to *Jannah* when we are sinners? We should repent and believe in Allah's mercy. Allah is *ar-Raḥman*. We are humans hence we are bound to sin but the best of us are the ones who repent. We have to know what kind of sins are there—the levels and categories of sin (major & minor). Allah uses different words for different sins in the Qur'an. After knowing what kind of sins there are, we have to realise the ones we do and repent. We should self-reflect, self-critique and have the self-control to avoid doing sins. Turn to Allah and believe in His love and mercy.

Every day we should ask our Lord, the Most Merciful,

that He grants us the straight path—or *sirat*—when we perform our *salah* (prayer) when we recite al-Fatiḥah. So keep praying and make lots of *du'a'* (invocation) to ask Allah (s.w.t.) to guide us to the *Siraṭal-Mustaqim*, the straight path, the clear, wide, welcoming and direct path to success peace and faith.

Yahya Ibrahim

Part 1:
What is the
Ultimate Goal?

Chapter 1: *Jannah is the Goal*

Let us begin with *Jannah.*

Allah (s.w.t.) emphasises to us the importance of being those who lead towards *Jannah.* One of the first instructions of the Prophet Muḥammad (s.a.w.) to those who succeeded him in spreading the words of faith to those the likes of Muʿadh ibn Jabal, ʿAli ibn Abi Ṭalib (r.a.), Abu Bakr as-Ṣiddiq (r.a.), ʿIkrima ibn Abi Jahl, ʿAmr ibn Hisham is:

The Prophet (s.a.w.) said,

"Make things easy for the people, and do not make it difficult for them, and make them calm (with glad tidings) and do not repulse (them).

(Ṣaḥih al-Bukhari 6125)

The Prophet (s.a.w.) gave the following advice to the people who will carry and spread the faith of Allah (s.w.t.) after he (s.a.w.) is gone. The Prophet (s.a.w.) advised us to always give glad tidings and to not repel people, as well as to make things easy and not difficult. The Prophet (s.a.w.) tells us to invite people to that which they recognise as good and ease, to not drive people away; to not make the people's circumstances difficult to the point that we become the obstacle of a person's response achieving return and upliftment in their relationship with Allah (s.w.t.).

I would like to mention another hadith that was a life-changing hadith for me. It changed my trajectory in my call to Allah and in my way of seeking to mentor the young as they grow older. One of my passions in life is to be part of an Islamic, especially in the West, hence one of the things that I centre the most is on the young hearts—to help shade the young hearts of Allah's mercy.

One of the interesting things about the Prophet (s.a.w.) was that he was a gifted storyteller. He would teach Islam not just by saying that "This is halal." "This is haram." "Do this." and "Do that." The teaching of the Prophet (s.a.w.) was not just command-based. Sometimes he would begin with "Did you know, back in the day, this happened." and "What do you think of these lessons that can be learned from the incident?" This is an example of just one of the occasions. To be specific most of these kinds of hadith begin with "Amongst the nations before you..."

Abu Hurayrah reported God's messenger (s.a.w.) as saying:

"There were two men among the B. Israil who loved one another, 'one of whom engaged ardently in worship while the other called himself a sinner. The former began to say, "Refrain from what you are doing," and the other would reply, "Let me

be alone with my Lord." One day he found him committing a sin which he considered serious and said, "Refrain;" to which he replied, "Let me be alone with my Lord. Were you sent to watch over me?" He then said, "I swear by God that God will never pardon you, nor will He bring you into paradise." God then sent to them an angel who took their spirits, and they came together into His presence. To the sinner He said, "Enter paradise by my mercy;" and to the other He said, "Can you forbid my mercy to my servant?" He replied, "No, my Lord." Then He said, "Take him away to hell."

(Mishkat al-Maṣabiḥ 2347)

In the time before our time, in the generation before us, they were two young men who were not blood brothers but they loved each other as if they were blood brothers. They were extremely close to each other. The Prophet (s.a.w.) described one of them as *ṣalih* (pious), as being outwardly righteous. The fact that the Prophet (s.a.w.) uses that word—*ṣalih*—shows that indeed that person is a good and righteous man. The man does what is expected; he prays, does the *siyam* (fast), gives *zakat*, and fulfils his obligations to his family and neighbours. On the other hand, his best friend is *muqsir*. It is the polite way of saying that he is a sinner.

The righteous one finds it easy to do the obligations of Allah (s.w.t.). The Prophet (s.a.w.) further mentions that whenever he, the *ṣaliḥ* one, (s.a.w.) his best friend—someone he was loyal to, someone he loved and cared for and wanted only good for—he would say to him to stop his wrongdoing or Allah (s.w.t.) will never forgive him. That if he, the *muqṣir*, were to keep on the wrong path, he would then have no hope in *Jannah*. His best friend was a believer who was a step behind.

We all have someone around us who are a step behind as well. We have within our families, neighbours, communities and nations. His best friend is a believer. His heart submits to Allah (s.w.t.) but his body is a step behind. That is the description by the Prophet (s.a.w.). *Muqṣir*—the person who can still improve and change. The best friend would say to leave him to Allah (s.w.t.) as Allah did not appoint his friend as a watcher over him, as a criticiser and condemner that whom at every step and movement of him is criticised. He tells his righteous friend that Allah did not appoint him as the policeman of his life.

The Prophet (s.a.w.) further foreshadows the Day of Judgement in the hadith of these two brothers. When they die, Allah will cause them both to be gathered together on the Day of Judgement and they will be questioned together. Allah will ask the righteous friend,

"Did you used to say to this man that I will not forgive him?"

"That I will not give him a place in *Jannah*?"

"Did I give my power to you?"

"Or did I give you the record of who will be going to *Jannah* and who won't?"

"Did I make you the one who can decide?"

"Witness now my forgiveness. I have forgiven this man of his sins. However, you, the righteous one, are to be held back."

The *ṣaliḥ*, the righteous, the one whose deeds are fulfilled and active in good, is held back as they are not enough to save him in an absolute sense without him being purged and cleansed for putting Allah's servants' hearts in despair. The Prophet (s.a.w.) then recites Allah's words:

$$\text{۞ قُـلْ يَـٰعِبَادِىَ ٱلَّذِيـنَ أَسْـرَفُواْ عَلَـىٰٓ أَنفُسِـهِمْ لَا تَقْنَطُـواْ مِـن رَّحْمَـةِ ٱللَّهِ ۚ إِنَّ ٱللَّـهَ يَغْفِـرُ ٱلذُّنُـوبَ جَمِيعًـا ۚ إِنَّهُ هُـوَ ٱلْغَفُـورُ ٱلرَّحِيـمُ ۝}$$

Say, "O' My servants who have transgressed against themselves [by sinning], do not despair of the mercy of Allah. Indeed, Allah forgives all sins. Indeed, it is He who is the Forgiving, the Merciful."

(az-Zumar, 39:53)

Allah (s.w.t.) refers to us as sinners who at times have committed errors, atrocities, and mistakes. Allah calls out to His servants who have transgressed, broken boundaries, jumped the fences, fallen into the pit, harmed themselves and are detrimental in their attitudes to not despair in His mercy.

Our purpose is *Jannah*.

This hadith is a foundation for us to begin reclassifying how we engage with those who we love, with those who at times are a step behind us or with a spouse who is not yet committed to the *fajr*. How do we engage with someone who is struggling with their hijab, with their choice of friend, with their financial aspects, that may not always be in the way of pleasing Allah? How do we engage with someone who we know their heart has love for Allah (s.w.t.) and the Messenger (s.a.w.) but the *dunya* (world), at times, overwhelms them?

Abu Miḥjan al-Thaqafi (r.a.)

Abu Miḥjan al-Thaqafi (r.a.) was one of the great *ṣaḥabah* of the Prophet (s.a.w.). He is one of those names that you

don't actually hear often. However, when you do, you will never forget. Abu Miḥjan had two great values. He was an eloquent poet and a fierce warrior. When he entered into Islam, he entered with his drunkenness. He was taken over by alcoholism and had the inability to cast it aside unlike the other *saḥabah* like Sayyidina 'Umar (r.a.) and Ibn Mas'ud who were able to turn over their liquor into the streets of Madinah.

Narrated Anas:

The Prophet (s.a.w.) ordered somebody to announce that: Abu Talha said to me, "Go out and see what this voice (this announcement) is." I went out and (on coming back) said, "This is somebody announcing that alcoholic beverages have been prohibited." Abu Talha said to me, "Go and spill it (i.e. the wine)," Then it (alcoholic drinks) was seen flowing through the streets of Madinah. At that time the wine was Al-Fadikh. The people said, "Some people (Muslims) were killed (during the battle of Uḥud) while wine was in their stomachs." So Allah revealed: "On those who believe and do good deeds there is no blame for what they ate (in the past)." (5.93)

(Ṣaḥiḥ al-Bukhari 4620)

The liquor was spilled onto the streets of Madinah, and the people were able to overcome the test of the prohibition of *khamr* (intoxicants) with one verse of the Qur'an:

$$\text{لَيْسَ عَلَى ٱلَّذِينَ ءَامَنُوا۟ وَعَمِلُوا۟ ٱلصَّٰلِحَٰتِ جُنَاحٌ فِيمَا طَعِمُوٓا۟ إِذَا مَا ٱتَّقَوا۟ وَّءَامَنُوا۟ وَعَمِلُوا۟ ٱلصَّٰلِحَٰتِ ثُمَّ ٱتَّقَوا۟ وَّءَامَنُوا۟ ثُمَّ ٱتَّقَوا۟ وَّأَحْسَنُوا۟ ۗ وَٱللَّهُ يُحِبُّ ٱلْمُحْسِنِينَ ۝٩٣}$$

There is not upon those who believe and do righteousness [any] blame concerning what they have eaten [in the past] if they [now] fear Allah and believe and do righteous deeds, and then fear Allah and believe, and then fear Allah and do good; and Allah loves the doers of good.

(al-Ma'idah, 5:93)

When it was instructed by Allah (s.w.t.) that they should leave the *khamr*, they all obeyed. However, there were some who kept it a secret in their home, and at times the secret would show itself in their public life through a scent, an inebriated comment, a moment of stumble—moments that would make people ponder and recognise that something

was off. During the time of the Prophet (s.a.w.), Abu Mihjan was held accountable for his actions. In the *khilafah* (Islamic state under the leadership of a Khalifa) of Abu Bakr (r.a.), he was held accountable and punished for his public drunkenness. In the *khilafah* of 'Umar al-Khattab (r.a.), he was held accountable and was publicly censored for his actions. Abu Mihjan was held accountable even until the Battle of al-Qadisiyyah. This is an important part. Let's see how close *Jannah* can be to someone's heart. Prior to the Battle of al-Qadisiyyah, Abu Mihjan brought along with him a secret stash of his liquor to the war. He brought it amongst the soldiers of Allah—the callers of Allah (s.w.t.) who are seeking Him, who are seeking *Jannah*. They were going to face an insurmountable Army of Persians, who was coming towards them. At a decisive moment in the middle of the night when everyone was resting for the battle the next day, praying their *tahajjud* (night prayer), making their *dhikr*, and reading the Qur'an—Abu Mihjan was drinking. When dawn arrived and the soldiers were preparing themselves for the insurmountable force, in the battle, Abu Mihjan was publicly shamed for his sin. Under the command of one of the ten companions whom *Jannah* is guaranteed—the *al-'Ashara al-Mubashsharūn*—Sa'd ibn Abi Waqqaṣ (r.a.) had ordered for Abu Mihjan to be tied to a tree due to his sin. Sa'd ibn Abi Waqqaṣ said that " I don't have time to deal with him right now. Tie him to the tree until the battle ends. We will discuss this matter after the battle. Abu Miḥjan cannot be in the same ranks as the believers. We have never defeated our enemies by number, superiority, and weaponry but we have defeated them on the account of the cleanliness of our hearts and the purpose of our deeds. Thus, put Abu Miḥjan away from the rest of us."

In his slumber, in his drunkenness, Abu Miḥjan wakes up to find that the army of the believers are descending into the valley for battle and the only people around him were the women, the nurses and the wife of Saʻd ibn Abi Waqqaṣ. Abu Miḥjan started to scream and cry out "Untie me. Let me go please." However, the women told him that they could not let him go as they had been ordered to keep him there. Abu Miḥjan then says "I swear to you by Allah, that if you untie me, I will wear armour that is not my armour. I will hold a sword and a shield that is not my own. I will cover my face so that I will not be recognised. And I will show you against the enemy of God, what will be pleasing to Allah (s.w.t.) and His Messenger (s.a.w.). If I remain alive, I will come back and tie myself to the tree." Thus, on that condition, he was let go.

It was at this critical moment; the Persian army was repelling the advance of the Muslims. The tide was turning against our *ummah* (community). At that moment, fearlessly entered Abu Miḥjan who was mounted on a horse that was not his own, who was in armour that was not his own, and who had a shield and sword that was not his own. He entered and cut right through the ranks of the army until he arrived at the centre and single handedly brought an end to those who were the bodyguards of the general. This then caused terror in the ranks of the enemy. And so, for that reason the Muslims were able to pull themselves and receive victory. Bleeding, wounded and alive, Abu Miḥjan came back and tied himself to the tree. When Saʿd ibn Abi Waqqaṣ (r.a.) came back and saw him, he said that he recognised that it was none other than Abu Miḥjan due to his skills. Saʿad ibn Abi Waqqaṣ (r.a.) said to Abu Miḥjan that "When we saw you descend into the valley; we knew it was nobody other than you. Nobody fights like you." And so Sayyidina Saʿd untied him and said that he will not question him about his last sin. He told Abu Miḥjan "Get up, for by Allah I will never flog you for drinking wine again." Abu Miḥjan then spoke words of poetry. He said, "It was not your chains that had tied me, it was my sin that tied me. And I will never be tied up with it again." "By Allah, I will never drink it again."

Sometimes letting a person be able to do something that is righteous by giving them the space to be able to redeem themselves— is the answer to them being able to find their path to *Jannah*.

Chapter 2: The Unseen is Real

Jannah is the goal. If we are not living for *Jannah*, then we are living for the *dunya*. If we are living for the *dunya*, then when the *dunya* ends—that is it. If we are living for the beyond, if we are the ones who understand that there is an unseen—if we are the ones who do not just believe but understand that there is an unseen, then it will lead us to the next stage. It will cause us to be the ones who are seeking to purify our life.

Notice here the usage of the word **understanding** that there is an unseen and not only believing in it. The word belief at times can mean different things to different people

يَعْلَمُ مُتَقَلَّبَكُمْ وَمَثْوَىٰكُمْ ﴿١٩﴾

So know, [O' Muḥammad], that there is no deity except Allah and ask forgiveness for your sin and for the believing men and believing women. And Allah knows of your movement and your resting place.

(Muḥammad, 47:19)

Allah (s.w.t.) uses the word *fa'lam,* meaning know. Thus, know, understand, comprehend, study, and deliberate over that there is none that is worthy of worship but Allah. That will lead us to the next stage and it will cause us to be among the ones who are seeking to purify our life and that of the believers and upon the *ummah* of Muḥammad (s.a.w.).

The unseen world is real. Allah (s.w.t.) introduces to us the Qur'an as the manual of guidance because that is what we asked of Him. We asked Allah in *surah* al-Fatiḥah:

$$\text{اَهْدِنَا ٱلصِّرَٰطَ ٱلْمُسْتَقِيمَ ۝}$$

Guide us to the straight path-

(al-Fatiḥah 1:6)

On the first page of the Qur'an, in the first opening *surah*, our first *du'a'* that we are asked to make is asking Allah to guide us to the straight path. And so Allah says to turn the page and He gives us His answer:

$$\text{ذَٰلِكَ ٱلْكِتَٰبُ لَا رَيْبَ ۛ فِيهِ ۛ هُدًى لِّلْمُتَّقِينَ ۝}$$
$$\text{ٱلَّذِينَ يُؤْمِنُونَ بِٱلْغَيْبِ وَيُقِيمُونَ ٱلصَّلَوٰةَ وَمِمَّا}$$
$$\text{رَزَقْنَٰهُمْ يُنفِقُونَ ۝}$$

This is the Book about which there is no doubt, a guidance for those conscious of Allah, who believe

in the unseen, establish prayer, and spend out of what We have provided for them,

(al-Baqarah, 2:2-3)

Allah says that we will find in this book, the Qur'an the guidance that we are asking for. The Qur'an will be that guidance for only those whose hearts are seeking purity, however. It is the guidance to those who approach the Qur'an with a sense of awe, who are attaining to it, and wanting to see the truth in it but not for those who are already in denial of it.

Allah (s.w.t.) further mentions in the third verse about the *ghaib* (the unseen)—that the guidance is for those who believe in the unseen. The unseen is Allah (s.w.t.), the angels, the scripture, the messengers, the Day of Judgement and *al-Qadr* (predestination). The guidance is for those who testify in regards to the unseen—they believe that:

there is more than what is in front of
them today,

there is more than what their feet are
grounded to today,

there is more than what is material in their
life today,

there is more than what the eyes see,

there is more than what the hand touches.

We must believe that there is an unseen, there is a world that is beyond our world, and there is a judgement greater than our judgement.

Belief in the unseen is what allows us to be those who are willing to get up and establish the prayer when there is no logical reason to do so—to get up without reason when everybody is asleep before the sun rises, each and every day. One of the annoying things back home for me is that I have a neighbour who has two dogs. It is not the dogs that I have problems with, it is just that they are always ahead of me in the morning. So the thing with dogs is that when they got to go, they got to go. Hence, the dogs built a routine in their master that he should be awake at 5 AM in the morning to take them out for a walk so that they can do their business. And the dogs will do whatever it takes for the master to quickly let them go out—scratch the door, jump on the bed, bark. And because of this, my neighbour is power walking at 5 AM. On the contrary, many of us are struggling to even get up for our *Fajr*, and what more for *tahajjud*. My neighbour wakes up **for an animal**. He wakes up committed each and every day while we, on the other hand, can't even wake up for *Jannah*. Unfortunately, there are some of us who do not see the value of *ṣalah* because it is not immediate. It is the thing that is not seen—so it is not present, and it cannot be felt unless you can absorb it in your heart. Of the most important inoculations or vaccines for our *akhirah* are to seek to establish a greater commitment to what is unseen of us.

Sometimes I did not understand this one hadith by the Prophet (s.a.w.):

> Be prompt in doing good deeds (before you are overtaken) by turbulence which would be like a part of the dark night. During (that stormy period) a man would be a Muslim in the morning and an unbeliever in the evening or he would be a believer in the evening and an unbeliever in the morning, and would sell his faith for worldly goods.
>
> (Ṣaḥiḥ Muslim 118)

The Prophet (s.a.w.) mentions a person who wakes up as a Muslim but at the end of the day he becomes *kafir* (disbeliever); that by the end of the day, something may occur that will cause the relinquishment of some of their *iman* (faith). They enter into a denial of sorts. May Allah (s.w.t.) not harm or test us in regard to this and may He always protect us.

Imagine, we begin our day happy and healthy with our family who is all well. Everything goes according to order for us but suddenly by *'Asr* there is perhaps a tragedy. Perhaps there would be someone who would fall to the ground in despair and say, "O' Allah why has this happened to me? What have we done wrong? I pray, fast and give *ṣadaqah*. I have never cheated or hurt anyone. Why?"

I personally have sat around with people who at that moment they wake up *mu'minin* (believer) and by the end of the day, if they are struggling, they question Allah as to why such despair has befallen them. So, visit your *iman*. The Prophet (s.a.w.) said in a hadith that *iman* tarnishes in the heart:

> Ibn 'Umar reported God's messenger as saying, "These hearts become rusty just as iron does when water gets to it." On being asked what could clear them he replied, "A great amount of remembrance of death and recitation of the Qur'an."

> (Mishkat al-Maṣabiḥ 2168)

The way our clothing becomes worn out, the same goes for our *iman*. The more we wash it, dry it, iron it, wear it, the more the *iman* fades away from the heart—when we forget and ignore our commitment to Allah. The more we use our *iman*, the more we think "I've just relied on my *iman* and I didn't fix it up, I didn't sew it up when there was a hole—when there was a question, I didn't get an answer to." Instead of it being a small cut, it becomes a rip in our faith. For example, our children ask us a simple question but we leave it unanswered, so it becomes a tear in the fabric of their *iman*.

Abdullah ibn Amr reported: The Messenger of Allah, peace and blessings be upon him, said, "Verily, the faith of one of you will wear out within him, just as a shirt becomes worn out, so ask Allah to renew faith in your hearts."

(al-Muʻjam al-Kabir lil-Ṭabarani 14668)

A part of the *ghaib*, the unseen is that *iman* in *Jannah*—the *iman* in the unseen. Believing and understanding the unseen is renewing our *iman* and commitment to Allah.

Chapter 3:
The Promise of Allah is True

How do we establish the recommitment to our *iman*? It is by recognising that the promise of Allah (s.w.t.) is true:

$$\text{إِنَّ وَعْدَ ٱللَّهِ حَقٌّ}$$

'Indeed, the promise of Allah is truth

(al-Jathiyah, 45:32)

I mentioned people who would fall to the ground in despair and question Allah as to why the tragedy has struck them when they have given their best to Allah. The thing is, who told you and I that just because we do good, we will only receive that which is good? Is that what Allah had promised us? Allah says:

$$\text{وَلَنَبْلُوَنَّكُم بِشَىْءٍ مِّنَ ٱلْخَوْفِ وَٱلْجُوعِ وَنَقْصٍ مِّنَ}$$
$$\text{ٱلْأَمْوَٰلِ وَٱلْأَنفُسِ وَٱلثَّمَرَٰتِ ۗ وَبَشِّرِ ٱلصَّٰبِرِينَ ﴿١٥٥﴾}$$
$$\text{ٱلَّذِينَ إِذَآ أَصَٰبَتْهُم مُّصِيبَةٌ قَالُوٓا۟ إِنَّا لِلَّهِ وَإِنَّآ إِلَيْهِ}$$
$$\text{رَٰجِعُونَ ﴿١٥٦﴾}$$

And We will surely test you with something of fear and hunger and a loss of wealth and lives and fruits, but give good tidings to the patient, Who, when disaster strikes them, say, "Indeed we belong to Allah, and indeed to Him we will return."

(al-Baqarah, 2:155-156)

The promise of Allah is true. Allah says that he will test us in this life. Allah says that there will be things that we love and we will be deprived of it by Him such as wealth, health, family, and the fruits of life. However, Allah also mentions at the end of the verse that He will give good news to those who in the moment of a calamity, they can be resilient. They can be tough, faithful, persevere and they can hold on and be patient. Their immediate response is we all belong to Allah (s.w.t.). Allah does of us as he wills, as a measure of life. We do not question the ultimate wisdom of the All-Wise, the Almighty Allah:

$$\text{لَا يُسْأَلُ عَمَّا يَفْعَلُ وَهُمْ يُسْأَلُونَ ﴿٢٣﴾}$$

He is not questioned about what He does, but they will be questioned.

(al-Anbiya', 21:23)

What we have to reflect on here is in regard to our natural response.

The promise of Allah is true.

The promise of Allah was not that if we maintain our *ṣalah*, we will have an easy life.

The promise of Allah was not that if we give *zakat*, He will increase us in prosperity.

The promise of Allah was not that if we hide the mistakes of others, people will not talk negatively about us then.

That was never the promise of Allah, but the promise of Allah is true which is He will give ease to those who experience hardship:

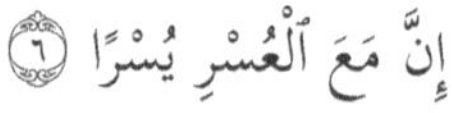

Indeed, with hardship [will be] ease.

(ash-Sharḥ, 94:6)

Allah says that when He tests us and we show *riḍa* (contentment), He will give us ease. That is Allah's promise. Ibn Qayyim also speaks about this matter. He mentions that the moment the believer shows *riḍa* when Allah tests them, He (s.w.t.) looks into our hearts. When Allah sees contentment, Allah allows the test to maintain, in order to see whether the *riḍa* is there just in the first strike or it will be with us along the journey. When Allah sees the *riḍa* as the overwhelming capacity of our heart, He will then raise the *balaʿ* (affliction). Allah will move it away. That is Allah's promise and Allah's promise is true.

Chapter 4: *Jannah is Worth the Struggle*

The struggle for *Jannah* is real and *Jannah* is worth for it. *SubḥanAllāh*, *Jannah* is worth it. It is worth our life. It is worth our wealth. It is worth giving off and leaving off some of what we enjoy in this *dunya*. *Jannah* is worth the temporary for the eternal. *Jannah* is worth it to allow us to be in the company of Allah, the company of the Prophet (s.a.w.) and the company of the righteous. *Jannah* is worth the three minutes of *Fajr*. It is worth waking up to do *ʿibadah* (worship) with the help of perhaps a sip of coffee to regain energy for it.

Jannah is worth in dignifying ourselves and ending haram relationships. *Jannah* is worth giving an inheritance that we had taken to the rightful owner who has the claim for it that we had took upon and were inflexible in. *Jannah* is worth to make us push beyond the injustices that have been inflicted upon us by others—by showing better in return than what we had received. *Jannah* is worth in us separating from the things that we love the most—in terms of our wants—so that instead we can help others with what they need.

Jannah is worth all of that.

Chapter 5:
The Trade of
Life

Allah mentions in the Qur'an about the seal that we have made as a trade in this life:

$$ ۞ إِنَّ ٱللَّهَ ٱشْتَرَىٰ مِنَ ٱلْمُؤْمِنِينَ أَنفُسَهُمْ وَأَمْوَٰلَهُم بِأَنَّ لَهُمُ ٱلْجَنَّةَ ... ﴿١١١﴾ $$

Indeed, Allah has purchased from the believers their lives and their properties [in exchange] for that they will have Paradise. They fight in the cause of Allah, so they kill and are killed. [It is] a true promise [binding] upon Him in the Torah and the Gospel and the Qur'an. And who is truer to his covenant than Allah? So rejoice in your transaction which you have contracted. And it is that which is the great attainment.

(at-Tawbah, 9:111)

Allah (s.w.t.) purchases from the believers their life and wealth. In return, Allah tells us that He will give us *Jannah*. What an amazing and great trade. What an amazing way of doing business to achieve the everlasting blessings of *Jannah*. The trade is that is lasting with Allah, as compared to that which is temporal and instantaneously regretful at times—the *dunya*—where we seek the *dunya* at the expense of the *akhirah*.

Part 2:

What is Sin?

Chapter 6:
A Human Condition

Sins are not the biggest problem in our life. Most people, their endeavour is to never make sin. That is why sometimes parents for instance make the mistake that the best thing from children is them being goody two shoes—a child who just sits quietly while smiling in a way that makes you wonder what is wrong with them, or whether they are alright.

The thing is, all of us are sinners but the best of us are the ones who acknowledge our sins and mistakes and repent. Initially, all of the *sahabah* were sinners in their life. 'Umar ibn al-Khaṭṭab (r.a.) was ferocious. Khalid ibn al-Walid (r.a.) was ferocious. 'Amr ibn al-'Aṣ was ferocious. Abu Bakr as-Ṣiddiq (r.a.) was a rebel. He (r.a.) would go to the marketplace and buy the weakest and the poorest slave with his wealth. Afterwards, when he went home, his father, Abu Quhafa would say "What have I done to deserve you? You have no mind for business, son. You went to the market and bought these weak men and weak women. They are worthless and you're paying more than they're due." Abu Bakr (r.a.) would rebel and say that it is because he wants to do it. Hence, there was constant angst between him (r.a.) with his father.

On the other hand, the father of 'Umar ibn al-Khaṭṭab used to be extremely upset with him. His father would force 'Umar (r.a.) out into the desert to tend to the camels.

His father, Al-Khaṭṭab ibn Nufayl would say to him that "I don't want to see your face so go out for forty days with these camels." 'Umar (r.a.) responded that they had slaves who could do the job but his father was reluctant. He said to 'Umar (r.a.), "No. This is where I want you to be. I don't want you here with me." This was due to the grief 'Umar (r.a.) had caused to his father.

All of the *ṣaḥabah* were sinners in their life initially, but they became the best as they became those who learned to control the beast that was within them. Thus the reformed sinner is the one who learns to control sin, learns to adapt themselves in being better and understands that we are all sinners. The Prophet (s.a.w.) said in a hadith:

> "Every son of Adam sins, and the best of the sinners are the repentant."

(Jamiʿ at-Tirmidhi 2499)

Every human being has that capacity for sin. However, the best sinner is the one who returns to Allah. The irony is that all of us who each have our own vast capacity and share of sin, are extremely good at hiding it. We are very good at masking, altering, negating, or even pretending that our sin is not there. The *ṣaḥabah* were petrified when the following verse of *surah* al-Baqarah were revealed. Allah said:

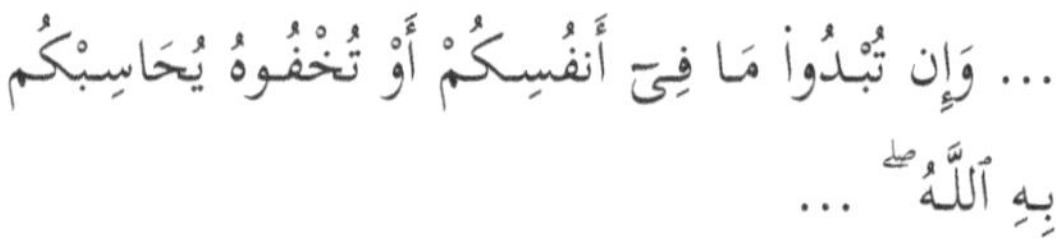

... وَإِن تُبْدُواْ مَا فِىٓ أَنفُسِكُمْ أَوْ تُخْفُوهُ يُحَاسِبْكُم بِهِ ٱللَّهُ ...

...Whether you show what is within yourselves or conceal it, Allah will bring you to account for it...

(al-Baqarah, 2:284)

Whether we keep the mistake in our heart and mind or make it known, Allah will hold us accountable for it. The *saḥabah* said to the Prophet (s.a.w.) that what had been revealed from the following verses were something that they cannot live with. They were afraid because what was in their mind would hold them accountable. They said "I didn't say anything. I didn't say anything when he/she walked into the room. Is Allah going to hold me accountable for what is in my head against me?" And so, Allah revealed the last two verses of *surah* al-Baqarah to answer their fears. Allah says:

لَا يُكَلِّفُ ٱللَّهُ نَفْسًا إِلَّا وُسْعَهَا ۚ لَهَا مَا كَسَبَتْ وَعَلَيْهَا مَا ٱكْتَسَبَتْ ۗ رَبَّنَا لَا تُؤَاخِذْنَآ إِن نَّسِينَآ أَوْ أَخْطَأْنَا ۚ رَبَّنَا وَلَا تَحْمِلْ عَلَيْنَآ إِصْرًا كَمَا حَمَلْتَهُۥ عَلَى ٱلَّذِينَ مِن قَبْلِنَا ۚ رَبَّنَا وَلَا تُحَمِّلْنَا مَا لَا طَاقَةَ لَنَا بِهِۦ ۖ وَٱعْفُ عَنَّا وَٱغْفِرْ لَنَا وَٱرْحَمْنَآ ۚ أَنتَ مَوْلَىٰنَا فَٱنصُرْنَا عَلَى ٱلْقَوْمِ ٱلْكَٰفِرِينَ ۝

Allah does not charge a soul except [with that within] its capacity. It will have [the consequence of] what [good] it has gained, and it will bear [the consequence of] what [evil] it has earned. "Our Lord, do not impose blame upon us if we have forgotten or erred. Our Lord, and lay not upon us a burden like that which You laid upon those before us. Our Lord, and burden us not with that which we have no ability to bear. And pardon us; and forgive us; and have mercy upon us. You are our protector, so give us victory over the disbelieving people."

(al-Baqarah, 2:286)

Ultimately, Allah is the master. He (s.w.t.) is the one in charge. We can only ask Him to let us stray from the path of sins and go unto the straight. Sin is a human condition; we have the capacity to make mistakes because it is something that we have been given the capacity of by Allah. Thus, we make *du'a'* to Him to seek his help and repent.

In an authentic hadith by Imam Bukhari, Musa (a.s.) was furious with Adam (a.s.):

> The Prophet (s.a.w.) said, "Adam and Moses argued with each other. Moses said to Adam. 'O' Adam! You are our father who disappointed us and turned us out of Paradise.' Then Adam said to him, 'O' Moses! Allah favored you with His talk (talked to you directly) and He wrote (the Torah) for you with His Own Hand. Do you blame me for action which Allah had written in my fate forty years before my creation?' So Adam confuted Moses, Adam confuted Moses," the Prophet (s.a.w.) added, repeating the Statement three times.

> (Ṣaḥīh al-Bukhari 6614)

Musa (a.s.) (s.a.w.) Adam (a.s.) after his death. He said to Adam (a.s.) "Are you the man who took us out of *Jannah*? What were you thinking? Allah gave you *Jannah* and told you not to go near that tree but you did. Out of all the trees in *Jannah*, why did you have to go there?"

Sin is a human condition. Some *'ulama'* (scholars) tell us that the tree was no different from the other trees. It did not have fruits that were different from the other tree's fruits. It was not taller, or brighter or more luminous. It did not have a sign that said "Don't go near this tree." Allah just said **this** tree. However, there is this human condition. Imam ibn Taimiyyah (r.a.h.) and Imam al-Ghazali (r.a.h.) mentioned that if *shaytan* did not a whisper to Adam (a.s.), he would have still eaten from the tree. That is why when Adam (a.s.) makes *tawbah*, He says "**We** have wronged ourselves" instead of saying "O' Allah forgive me and my wife for *shaytan* tricking us." Adam says "we", that they are the ones who are wrong.

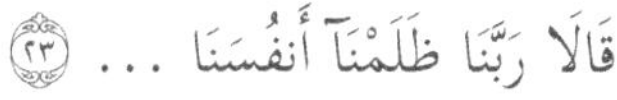

They said, "Our Lord, we have wronged ourselves...

(al-A'raf, 7:23)

It is us that have wronged ourselves. *Shaytan* is not the one who lets people sleep during *Fajr*. It is us. We love the bed, the comfort, and the air-conditioner and so we continue to sleep and miss our *Fajr*. *Shaytan* is probably be like: "Why do you keep blaming me? What did I do? This is all on you. It is your fault. I just made it easier for you. I just gave you a greater invitation, but the craving is from you."

The craving in doing the err is on us. We have the capacity to make that mistake. However, this also means that we have the ability and power to step back from sin as well. And so, Allah (s.w.t.) invites us to the challenge of life.

$$\text{ٱلَّذِى خَلَقَ ٱلْمَوْتَ وَٱلْحَيَوٰةَ لِيَبْلُوَكُمْ أَيُّكُمْ أَحْسَنُ عَمَلًا ۚ وَهُوَ ٱلْعَزِيزُ ٱلْغَفُورُ ﴿٢﴾}$$

[He] who created death and life to test you [as to] which of you is best in deed - and He is the Exalted in Might, the Forgiving -

(al-Mulk, 67:2)

Allah is the one who gives us life and death. He is the one who brings out death and gives life. And the test for those who have found life by Allah is in regards to our human condition—whether we will try and achieve better success or keep sinning. The test upon the human condition is that will we try to be better than we were yesterday; are we able to make our hearts inspired to be better than what it is today; are we willing to forgo, challenge, and push ourselves further to achieve the better and the greater in our tomorrow and subsequent days?

Chapter 7: Doubtful Arrogance VS Desirous Consumption

There are two branches of sin. All of the sins that we get involved in, come back to two categories—doubtful arrogance and desirous consumption. The first category is one of doubtful arrogance.

$$\text{وَمَآ أَظُنُّ ٱلسَّاعَةَ قَآئِمَةً وَلَئِن رُّدِدتُّ إِلَىٰ رَبِّى لَأَجِدَنَّ خَيْرًا مِّنْهَا مُنقَلَبًا ﴿٣٦﴾}$$

And I do not think the Hour will occur. And even if I should be brought back to my Lord, I will surely find better than this as a return."

(al-Kahf, 18:36)

The people in this category **do not think**. They assume that it is alright to miss their *Fajr* as it is only two *rak'ah*; that it is okay to miss *Fajr* because they will pray their *Zuhr, 'Aṣr, Maghrib, 'Isha'*; that it is alright because 80% of the time they pray. Hence, they think and say that Allah will forgive them.

There is this doubtful arrogance. We doubt the capacity of Allah to reward us greater than what we are given, and we doubt with arrogance the capacity of Allah to hold us accountable for what we deserve. The *kibr* (arrogance) becomes a central factor. Doubtful arrogance is what you see in *Iblis*. He knows Allah. That is why Allah (s.w.t.) begins with the story of the devil before the story of Adam (a.s.). In the Qur'an, the narrations about *Iblis* in *surah* al-Baqarah and al-A'raf of the Battle of *Iblis* against himself—whereby that then pushes himself into arrogance and against Allah, shows that Allah was gentle with him. We will find in those narrations that Allah was gentle in His words with *Iblis* as Allah asks him, *mā mana'aka*—"What stopped you?"

$$\text{قَالَ مَا مَنَعَكَ أَلَّا تَسْجُدَ إِذْ أَمَرْتُكَ ۖ قَالَ أَنَا خَيْرٌ مِّنْهُ خَلَقْتَنِى مِن نَّارٍ وَخَلَقْتَهُ مِن طِينٍ ﴿١٢﴾}$$

[Allah] said, "What prevented you from prostrating when I commanded you?" [Satan] said, "I am better than him. You created me from fire and created him from clay [i.e., earth]."

(al-A'raf, 7:12)

Iblis replies that it is because he is better, that is why he did not prostrate to Adam (a.s.). This shows his arrogance. He doubts the capacity of Allah holding him accountable. He says it is because He (s.w.t.) gave him the ability to choose. *Iblis* questions why Allah did not make him then like Jibril, who does as instructed. His arrogance denies that it isn't his fault for not prostrating. It is all because he is better and he is capable of choosing.

The second branch is desirous consumption. Adam (a.s.) wanted that tree. He wanted to have more. He wanted to have that pursuit of instantaneous gratification. When Adam went to the tree, *shayṭan* tips in and says something which becomes the final straw that breaks Adam's heart. *Shayṭan* simply says that the tree is a tree of eternality:

$$فَوَسْوَسَ إِلَيْهِ ٱلشَّيْطَـٰنُ قَالَ يَـٰٓأَادَمُ هَلْ أَدُلُّكَ عَلَىٰ شَـجَرَةِ ٱلْخُلْدِ وَمُلْكٍ لَّا يَبْلَىٰ ﴿١٢٠﴾$$

Then Satan whispered to him; he said, "O' Adam, shall I direct you to the tree of eternity and possession that will not deteriorate?"

(Ṭaha, 20:120)

The *shayṭan* whispers that the tree is the tree of eternity and also with it is the Kingdom that will not be lost, because nobody wants to live forever poor. Can you imagine living forever poor? You are 500 years old and still broke. You're still taking the bus and have no savings. So *shayṭan* is basically saying to Adam (a.s.) that "Live forever and be King. Nothing that you have will be taken away from you then." So, what is it then that Adam feared? What did he doubt? He doubted that the mercy of Allah (s.w.t.) will be long standing. Allah had told him and his wife to enjoy Paradise:

$$ ٱدْخُلُوا۟ ٱلْجَنَّةَ أَنتُمْ وَأَزْوَٰجُكُمْ تُحْبَرُونَ ٧٠ $$

Enter Paradise, you and your kinds, delighted."

(az-Zukhruf, 43:70)

He had a place in *Jannah* and he will be there forever but there was that moment where Adam wondered, "What if it ends? What if all that leaves?" Even though Allah mentioned to him that he can enjoy paradise but he (a.s.) at one point doubted the mercy of Allah and fell into his desires. Therefore, when these two things—doubtful arrogance and desirous consumption—come together, we will find ourselves in peril.

Chapter 8:
The Monsters Amongst Us

Islam is meant to be a natural way of life. It is meant to be without pretence and pretend. Whenever a person acts out Islam in a way that is different to what they are holding and building in their heart, they will then fall away from the path of truth. That is why the key to the *qalb* (heart) is the sunnah of the Prophet (s.a.w.). In the sunnah, the Prophet (s.a.w.) mentions that there is a part of the body that if it is healthy, then the rest of the body will be healthy as well—that is the *qalb*. The spiritual heart and the physical heart become a central focus. The Prophet (s.a.w.) says in a hadith:

> I heard Allah's Messenger (s.a.w.) saying
>
> ...Beware! There is a piece of flesh in the body if it becomes good (reformed) the whole body becomes good but if it gets spoilt the whole body gets spoilt and that is the heart.
>
> (Ṣaḥiḥ al-Bukhari 52)

Whenever our heart is distant from our actions, we become zombie-like.

Vampires, werewolves, and zombies are real. There are people who Allah describes in the Qur'an are like zombies, *aḥyain* (not alive). They are *amwātun ghayru aḥyain*, meaning they are dead without life:

أَمْوَٰتٌ غَيْرُ أَحْيَآءٍ ۖ وَمَا يَشْعُرُونَ أَيَّانَ يُبْعَثُونَ ﴿٢١﴾

They are [in fact] dead, not alive, and they do not perceive when they will be resurrected.

(an-Naḥl, 16:21)

These zombie-like people, walk around this earth breathing, eating, drinking, enjoying, living, earning, buying, and selling but they are dead.

أَوَمَن كَانَ مَيْتًا فَأَحْيَيْنَٰهُ وَجَعَلْنَا لَهُۥ نُورًا يَمْشِى بِهِۦ فِى ٱلنَّاسِ كَمَن مَّثَلُهُۥ فِى ٱلظُّلُمَٰتِ لَيْسَ بِخَارِجٍ مِّنْهَا ۚ كَذَٰلِكَ زُيِّنَ لِلْكَٰفِرِينَ مَا كَانُوا۟ يَعْمَلُونَ ﴿١٢٢﴾

And is one who was dead and We gave him life and made for him light by which to walk among the people like one who is in darkness, never to emerge therefrom? Thus it has been made pleasing to the disbelievers that which they were doing.

(al-Anʿam, 6:122)

Allah gives the example of the one who is dead and Allah gave them life. Allah gave them in their heart—faith.

Allah put in their hearts *nur* (light) and they begin to walk amongst mankind.

The living dead is a real phenomenon. Cognitive dissonance, on the other hand, is more of a science psychological term. Cognitive dissonance is when you know in your mind that what you are doing (actions) is not consistent with your values. It upsets you. It perturbs you. It keeps you awake at night. Cognitive dissonance is one of the greatest components in most people who do not have chemical reasons for mental health issues. They are living a life that is inconsistent with what they believe, with what they hold on to as the truth. They are the living dead.

The werewolves—on the other hand—are people who are very calm, and very happy, but when something happens, or when something does not go right, they become a ferocious beast. One little problem along the way in their life and they turn into snarling, angry beasts. They are foaming at the mouth—saying words that nobody imagined they could ever say. They were always well-mannered but suddenly their animalistic behaviour comes out after something goes wrong. It takes people by surprise. One moment we see them in the masjid being polite and caring but when they walk into their home, they change.

Vampires—they suck the life out of you. They drain you

of your *iman*, your good deeds, your reputable behaviour, and from Islam. They are the ones who want us to stay up at night. They are the ones who want to commune with others that are like them. They are the ones who huddle you away from the light.

These 'mythical creatures' are real beings. Allah further warns us of that deceptive, egotistical, defective understanding that leads to arrogance—which then pollutes one's heart. For instance, the love of material, the love of excess, and especially the love to be seen even in things that relate to Allah (s.w.t.) are of the most ruinous of affairs. The Prophet (s.a.w.) also says in a hadith:

> "The Messenger of Allah (s.a.w.) came out to us when we were discussing Dajjal (False Christ) and said: 'Shall I not tell you of that which I fear more for you than Dajjal?' We said: 'Yes.' He said: 'Hidden polytheism, when a man stands to pray and makes it look good because he sees a man looking at him.'"

> (Sunan ibn Majah 4204)

The Prophet said that one of the sins that he fears the most for his nations, for his *ummah* is that they will commit *shirk* (polytheism) in a minor capacity—in a hidden capacity. They are not worshipping idols. They are worshipping Allah, they are standing before Allah (s.w.t.) in their prayer, but they are conscious of those who look at them. They will make their prayer ever more devout, humble and beautiful because they saw the eyes of another fall upon them. *SubḥanAllāh.*

Let me give you an example. Perhaps you are at home with your three children. Every day when you are praying, you only read *surah* al-Ikhlaṣ. However, when somebody comes and visits you, when you have a guest, you as the Imam start to recite the prayer in a more beautiful and devout manner that it awes the other people.

We have this capacity that at times our hearts crave more than they should. This could be, of course, to our detriment. If used in the right and proper way, it most definitely could be a beautiful thing—when it is nurtured in the right way. When the Prophet (s.a.w.) saw somebody, who had the capacity to do something good, he (s.a.w.) would nurture that good in the. He (s.a.w.) would put it in a restrained manner but at the same time would increase them in that good thing.

An example of this can be observed in Zayd ibn Thabit. The Prophet (s.a.w.) told him to put down the sword and pick up the pen instead. The Prophet (s.a.w.) told him that he was not meant for the Battle of Badr and Uḥud. Zayd became the one who had the role of writing down the Qur'an verses that were sent to the Prophet (s.a.w.) and became one who was an expert in the Qur'an. 'Umar even once addressed the expert knowledge of the Qur'an that Zayd possessed. He said, "O people, whoever wants to ask about the Qur'an, let him go to Zayd ibn Thabit."

For Usama ibn Zayd, it was different. He became the one who led a battle. At that time, Usama ibn Zayd was a youth, a teenager. In the ranks of the army that he was leading, there was 'Umar ibn al-Khaṭṭab. *Masha'Allāh.* The Prophet (s.a.w.) said that he had a future in regard to that matter. It is even mentioned in a hadith:

> The Prophet (s.a.w.) appointed Usama as the commander of the troops (to be sent to Syria). The Muslims spoke about Usama (unfavorably). The Prophet (s.a.w.) said, "I have been informed that you spoke about Usama. (Let it be known that) he is the most beloved of all people to me."
>
> (Ṣaḥiḥ al-Bukhari 4468)

The heart is extremely important. Allah (s.w.t.) wants us to recognise that the place where sins begin is always in terms of intent. What makes a sin different from a mistake is the intent. We still ask Allah to forgive our mistakes, our *khaṭa* (error). However, the *khaṭa* that we make is not like the *sayyiah* (evil) that we choose. *Sayyiah* is an act of evil that is recognised by us and others. It is different from *khaṭa* which is a mistake that was made where we did not recognise its enormity, its sinfulness, its impact, its egregiousness. Perhaps when we did the *khaṭa* we thought, "It was something that I should not have done but I did not know that it was a very bad thing." Therefore, it is very important for us to know and understand the level, categories and habits of the sins—and to subsequently then correlate it to its effect upon our hearts and our demonstrated behaviour.

Chapter 9:
Levels of Knowledge

There are two levels of intentional knowledge that we have. One knowledge is accepted by all human beings—which is the knowledge of observation, the scientific method and the senses. We see, we hear, we touch, we feel things that we can recreate—and so we believe in it. However, for us as Muslims, we also believe in the *wahyu* (revelation) which is at times of greater importance than the observable and temporal in our life. This distinguishes us, Muslims from others. Recently, I went to the McDonald's in Malaysia with my family. My daughter said that the McDonald's here smells different than back home in Perth. I told her it is because they do not sell pork. It smells different as there is no *khinzir*. Why do we find offence with *lahm al-khinzir* or the flesh of swine? Is it because of a scientific reason? No, it is not really science.

If a pork chop and a lamb chop were cut in the same size and length, from a distance they look the same. They are meat or what the people back in Perth refer to as protein. They don't talk about meat anymore. They say 'protein'. And that is a stepping stone as well to giving us protein from insects as well. It is a mind shift. It is a paradigm shift. It is how they get people ready for protein because they all (lamb, pork, insects) are protein. It is the same. If we were to look at it from the lens of science, based on its muscle tissue then there is no distinctiveness between the lamb chop and the pork chop. There is no difference in them if they are both cooked well, harvested from clean animals, and free from contagion. There is no scientific reason to then say why those two types of meat are different on the menu. But actually, there is one reason to say that it is different. For us Muslims, there is a difference because we believe in the *waḥyu* as well, and not only the material knowledge. This is where Allah draws the line and He says "Adam don't go near that tree. Yahya don't eat that flesh." Allah draws the line for no reason. Thus, that is why Allah does not qualify the haram. The *ʿulamaʾ*; they try to give us reasons. They attempt to give us at times rational reasons, spiritual reasons, and *ḥikmah* (wisdoms) about it. And nobody would ever dare say this is **the** reason; that is only known to Allah. Allah does not qualify why it is haram. Allah simply says do not go near it, *ḥurrimat ʿalaykum:*

$$\text{حُرِّمَتْ عَلَيْكُمُ ٱلْمَيْتَةُ وَٱلدَّمُ وَلَحْمُ ٱلْخِنزِيرِ ... ﴿٣﴾}$$

Prohibited to you are dead animals, blood, the flesh of swine…

(al-Maʾidah, 5:3)

Allah just says that it is haram for us. When the instruction is given, our hearts control our minds. Allah says to believe in His instructions and obey. The heart has to believe and tell the mind to obey the order.

$$\ldots\; وَقَالُوا سَمِعْنَا وَأَطَعْنَا ۖ غُفْرَانَكَ رَبَّنَا وَإِلَيْكَ الْمَصِيرُ ﴿٢٨٥﴾$$

...And they say, "We hear and we obey. [We seek] Your forgiveness, our Lord, and to You is the [final] destination."

(al-Baqarah, 2:285)

Put aside the mentality of believing because of science, or because there is no real reason, or that it is a clean animal. No. Put that knowledge aside. We believe in the *waḥyu* as an essential element of diagnosing right from wrong, halal from haram; good from bad; righteous from immorality; blessed from deprived; light from darkness; wisdom from oppression; ease from discomfort; increase from decrease in the *deen* (religion); or increase from decrease in money or wealth.

This is an interesting point to note here. In the logical sense, it does not make sense that when we give from our wealth and money, our money will grow. However, in our *deen*, it is "give and it has not left from your pocket." This is what we believe as Muslims. What we consume and spend on ourselves is gone but when we give to another to help fulfil their need, it will remain and has been blessed. It is all in the *waḥyu,* in the revelation that is unseen. However, the effect of believing in the *waḥyu* becomes profound on our hearts.

Abu Umamah told of Abu Dharr asking God's Prophet (s.a.w.) to tell him what the reward for *ṣadaqah* would be, and receiving the reply,

"Many times as much, and more still with God."

(Mishkat al-Maṣabiḥ 1928)

Chapter 10: Levels, Categories & Habits of Sin

Types of Sins stated in the Qur'an

- A Slip (زلة)

- Reprehensible (جناح)

- Enormity (كبيرة)

- Negligence of family (حوب)

- Compilation (لمم)

- Delay and neglect of good (إثم)

- Burden (وزر)

- A humiliating consequence following behind you (ذنب)

- Mark (خطأ)

- Shame (سيئة)

- Public Oppression (بغي)

- Breaks promise (حنث)

- Evil Conduct (سوء العمل)

- Opposing command (عصى)

- Public indecency, & obscenity (فاحشة)

- Wrong oneself (ظلمنا نفسه)

- Darkness & Oppression (ظلم)

- Crossing the boundaries (فسق)

- Opposition (خالف)

- Pressure (مقتا)

- Condemnable (عيب)

- Recognised immorality (منكر)

Look at all the subtle words that are used to describe the sins. Usually, when we look at the English translation of the Qur'an, it will mention almost all the sins as sins instead of the specific word. This is where we can the eloquence of the language of the Qur'an, the eloquence of the words that Allah chose to preserve in the final testament to humanity.

1. A Slip (زلة)

Zallah means a slip. Let us say that I am walking, and then suddenly I slip. I was not looking properly and I was not paying attention to my surroundings, so I tripped. It was not intentional, but its effect could at times be greater. For instance, a person could slip off a mountain which will then cause them their death.

At times, when people look back at their past sins and mistakes, they say "it was just an accident, it was just a slip." The thing is, there are accidents that we make in our spiritual life that can have a serious effect. The accident can be terminal; an ending to a relationship; an ending to the *barakah* (blessing) in our homes or an ending to the spread of *khayr* (good).

A slip that Allah acknowledges as "just a slip" is something that is categorised for us in the Qur'an as a specific category of sin.

2. Reprehensible (جناح)

Allah usually says *walā junaḥā 'alaikum*—"There is no blame upon you"—that it is not reprehensible for you if you were to do certain things. We have this concept in our *shari'ah*—*al-*

asha'tu 'rif bi'addadiha—**things known by their opposites.** When a comparison is made between the right and wrong, we can see clearly the characteristics of reprehensible, and when a person is doing reprehensible things.

Let us have an example of a situation which could take place on a plane. So, for instance, if I were to say to a brother "do not stand" what I mean is to remain seated in his chair. I may not say "stay seated." Instead, I might say "please don't stand up" which also means stay seated. However, sometimes people don't listen.

Allah (s.w.t.) speaks about reprehensible things in the Qur'an. When Allah speaks about things in relation to *junah*, it is usually on personal interrelationships with others. It is usually about the things that we take as liberty with our loved ones; where at times we act reprehensibly and assume the other party who loves us will forgive us. For instance, our father, mother, spouse and friend. When we act reprehensibly, the damage is done to the other party. However, the person who acts reprehensibly, assumes that they will be forgiven for their behaviour because their loved ones have forgiven them in the past before. And so, because they have forgiven them in the past, they are sure that their loved ones will continue to forgive them even in the future.

3. Enormity (كبيرة)

Kabirah is one of the big sins. It is the one that we arrive at without knowing how we got there. There are these little things that will lead us away from the path of the *Ṣiraṭal-Mustaqim*. And when we wake up and look around, we wonder how we went there—how we went so far away from Allah (s.w.t.). We start to wonder then how we broke simple rules and now we find ourselves placed in a dangerous territory. Allah says:

$$\text{إِن تَجْتَنِبُوا۟ كَبَآئِرَ مَا تُنْهَوْنَ عَنْهُ نُكَفِّرْ عَنكُمْ سَيِّـَٔاتِكُمْ وَنُدْخِلْكُم مُّدْخَلًا كَرِيمًا ٣١}$$

If you avoid the major sins which you are forbidden, We will remove from you your lesser sins and admit you to a noble entrance [into Paradise].

(an-Nisa', 4:31)

Allah (s.w.t.) tells us that our small sins will be forgiven as long as we stay away from the *kabirah*. What are some of the *kabirah*?

The Messenger of Allah (s.a.w.) said: "Whoever comes worshipping Allah and not associating anything with Him, establishing *ṣalah*, paying *zakat* and avoiding major sins, Paradise will be his." They asked him about major sins and he said: "Associating others with Allah, killing a Muslim soul, and fleeing (from the battlefield) on the day of the march."

(Sunan an-Nasa'i 4009)

In the hadith, The Prophet (s.a.w.) says that the one who takes an equal partner or a share with Allah—which should only be for Allah—has committed *kabirah*. Even assuming that you are who you are today because of yourself and not Allah is also a *kabirah*. This is because you are saying that you are the one who has made yourself, that you are self-made as you invested in yourself to be better and smarter. Hence you end up associating yourself on the same level as Allah, you end up committing *shirk* because of your desire because you assume that you are the God of yourself. Allah says:

أَفَرَءَيْتَ مَنِ ٱتَّخَذَ إِلَـٰهَهُۥ هَوَىٰهُ وَأَضَلَّهُ ٱللَّهُ عَلَىٰ عِلْمٍ وَخَتَمَ عَلَىٰ سَمْعِهِۦ وَقَلْبِهِۦ وَجَعَلَ عَلَىٰ بَصَرِهِۦ غِشَـٰوَةً فَمَن يَهْدِيهِ مِنۢ بَعْدِ ٱللَّهِ ۚ أَفَلَا تَذَكَّرُونَ ﴿٢٣﴾

Have you seen he who has taken as his god his [own] desire, and Allah has sent him astray due to knowledge and has set a seal upon his hearing and his heart and put over his vision a veil? So who will guide him after Allah? Then will you not be reminded?

(al-Jathiyah, 45:23)

Allah asks whether we have considered the depravity of the ones who made themselves their own design their own God. Whatever they want, whatever their heart desires they will do it. Unfortunately, this is the type of liberalism that is called to today. We are called to ourselves. The ideology is made to seem that the desire of every human is to just be free. To be free to do what we want, when we want it, and who we want to be with for however long or short period of time. To be able to make their own choices because it is their life thus they want to live as they please as they only have this one chance.

Al'ishraku billah (to ascribe partners to Allah) is not just simply worshipping other than Allah. It is a mindset that pulls Allah out of the centre of our world, and out of the centre of our decision-making. It is a *kabirah*. Second to that is *'ququul walidayn* or a violation of duties towards the two parents. If we were to like at the structure where first and foremost, we must obey Allah (s.w.t.) commands as He is the Almighty. After Allah, we are told to obey our parents. Hence, we can see the structure of who we are to obey is Allah and then our parents. So, going against both Allah and our parents is a *kabirah*. There is this caveat that I would like to state as well. Not all of us are blessed with parents who deserve absolute devotion. Some of us are challenged by parents who are toxic. Some of us are challenged with parents who are immoral. Some of us are challenged with parents who were not present, who were not nurturing, loving, or faithful. They are even treacherous to our spouses. Some of us were and are still challenged with this. Therefore, when we speak about *'ququul walidayn*, Allah does not only talk about being good to our parents. Allah says not being unruly to your parents—meaning in what they deserve, in the capacity that they deserve. For some parents, the only thing they deserve is *Assalamu 'alaikum*, and *Eid Mubarak*. That is all. That is how much some can give from what they have experienced and from what they need to shelter in their home and family. A phone call to wish Eid Mubarak and *salam* or to tell them that you have sent some money into their account. That is it some us.

For others, on the other hand, The Prophet (s.a.w.) said in a hadith:

A man came to the Prophet (s.a.w.) and said:

Messenger of Allah, I have property and children, and my father finishes my property. He replied; You and your property belong to your father; your children come from the pleasantest of what you earn; so enjoy from the earning of your children.

(Sunan Abi Dawud 3530)

The Prophet (s.a.w.) says that all of our wealth belongs to our father. *SubḥanAllāh*. Thus, being unruly, disrespectful, and intentionally having abusive behaviour towards our parents, especially when they become defenceless is *'ququl walidayn*. It is a *kabirah*.

Other *kabirah* are also committing *zina* (illicit sexual relations) and murder. The *kabirah* can become infectious ailments in our homes, in our considerations towards those who have a right against us which can lead to *ḥawb* (negligence of family).

4. Negligence of family (حوب)

Ḥawb is *ḥūban kabīran*. When Allah (s.w.t.) uses that word, He is speaking directly about the negligence of one's responsibility to those who are in relation to us. One of the beautiful things about the Malay culture is the naming system—the use of *bin* and *binti*. That concept is Islam and as well as for us to be negligent of our duties to those who came before us and those who we are ordered to look after—the ones coming after us. Look at the two beautiful *du'a'* of Prophet Ibrahim (a.s.) :

$$رَبِّ ٱجْعَلْنِى مُقِيمَ ٱلصَّلَوٰةِ وَمِن ذُرِّيَّتِى ۚ رَبَّنَا وَتَقَبَّلْ دُعَآءِ ۞ رَبَّنَا ٱغْفِرْ لِى وَلِوَٰلِدَىَّ وَلِلْمُؤْمِنِينَ يَوْمَ يَقُومُ ٱلْحِسَابُ ۞$$

My Lord, make me an establisher of prayer, and [many] from my descendants. Our Lord, and accept my supplication. Our Lord, forgive me and my parents and the believers the Day the account is established."

(Ibrahim, 14:40-41)

Most *ulama'* say that these two *du'a'* must be done in tandem because they were made in tandem by the Prophet Ibrahim (a.s.). In verse forty, he (a.s.) is looking to the future of those who will come after him. He doesn't just make *du'a'* for his children who were with him, but he also makes *du'a'* for his descendants. He says *du'a'* for his *dhurriyyat* (offsprings), those who he has put forth as seeds into the world that would come after. He is making also making a *du'a'* for Muḥammad (s.a.w.) as well— the *dhurriyyat* that would come generations after. Through the verse, we can see the mindset of the believer who deems that what to come is more important than the past. Hence, he (a.s.) asks Allah to answer the first *du'a'* first. Afterwards, in verse forty-one, Prophet Ibrahim (a.s.) makes the second *du'a'* for those whose hearts have become dark.

Prophet Ibrahim (a.s.) is the one whose father had tied him up with his people. His father was the one who joined in catapulting him into a blazing pit of flame, to intend his death. His father is the one who Allah records his words in the Qur'an saying:

قَالَ أَرَاغِبٌ أَنتَ عَنْ ءَالِهَتِى يَـٰٓإِبْرَٰهِيمُ ۖ لَئِن لَّمْ تَنتَهِ لَأَرْجُمَنَّكَ ۖ وَٱهْجُرْنِى مَلِيًّا ﴿٤٦﴾

[His father] said, "Have you no desire for my gods, O' Abraham? If you do not desist, I will surely stone you, so avoid me a prolonged time."

(Maryam, 19:46)

His father told him to leave as he did not want to ever see him again—"avoid me a prolonged time." He said to Ibrahim (a.s.) that if he were to come in his way again he would stone him to death. That father is the one who Ibrahim says, *waighfirli abī,* "O' Allah forgive my father as he was one who was led astray."

$$ وَٱغْفِرْ لِأَبِىٓ إِنَّهُۥ كَانَ مِنَ ٱلضَّآلِّينَ ﴿٨٦﴾ $$

And forgive my father. Indeed, he has been of those astray.

(ash-Shu'ara', 26:86)

Prophet Ibrahim (a.s.) only stopped making this *du'a'* until it become certain with his father's death, that his father was no longer capable of receiving that *du'a'* and being of those who is going to be welcomed in *Jannah*.

5. Compilation (لمم)

Family is usually where we have *lamam* or compilations. Rarely, our interpersonal relationships break down on account of a one off. The *lamam* is the compiled small things that pile one on top of another. The *lamam* is the compilation of things that we had to put up with someone's behaviour, insolence, and vulgarity which lasted every day, every week, every month or even a year. All those things get piled up one on top of another until eventually the last little straw, one little particle breaks down everything.

6. Delay and neglect of good (إثم)

Ithm is not necessarily that we did something wrong, or vulgar but it is that our mistake was that there was an opportunity for good and we, however, intentionally backed away from it.

... وَمَن يَكْتُمْهَا فَإِنَّهُۥٓ ءَاثِمٌ قَلْبُهُۥ ۗ وَٱللَّهُ بِمَا تَعْمَلُونَ عَلِيمٌ ۝

… for whoever conceals it—his heart is indeed sinful, and Allah is Knowing of what you do.

(al-Baqarah, 2:283)

Allah talks about the one whose heart had an opportunity for good but his heart closed off into doing it. Sometimes we feel this after time has passed. We realise later the missed opportunity. Sometimes, it is an act of charity. Sometimes it is those moments that when we look back, we tell ourselves that we would have done it differently. For instance, an argument. Most of us wish that we could go back in time and not say certain words to the other party. We look back perhaps on a missed opportunity to apologise to someone who has already passed away. We knew that we had that opportunity to apologise but did not do it.

Therefore, *ithm* is not that we did wrong, but it is that we intentionally missed and wasted the opportunity to do good and Allah condemns that behaviour in the Qur'an.

7. Burden (وزر)

Allah warns us of the *wizr* ; the weight, the burden, the heaviness. The Prophet (s.a.w.) mentions that on the Day of Judgement, people will come carrying their burdens upon their shoulders. The heavier the burden, the tougher and slower the progression. Allah tells us in the Qur'an:

وَلَا تَزِرُ وَازِرَةٌ وِزْرَ أُخْرَىٰ ۚ ...﴿١٨﴾

And no bearer of burdens will bear the burden of another....

(Fatir, 35:18)

Allah also says that nobody will carry the burden of another.

... إِنَّ ٱلسَّمْعَ وَٱلْبَصَرَ وَٱلْفُؤَادَ كُلُّ أُولَـٰئِكَ كَانَ عَنْهُ مَسْـُٔولًا ﴿٣٦﴾

… Indeed, the hearing, the sight and the heart - about all those [one] will be questioned.

(al-Isra', 17:36)

Our *wizr* is heavy. Our hearing, sight, evil intentions, and whispers of the heart will all be questioned by Allah. The Prophet (s.a.w.) mentioned that the things that will light our road on the Day of Judgement are the things that fill our scale with good deeds. Imagine that there is a *mizan*, a balance, that we want to take out of the burden and to offset it with good deeds.

Sometimes our sins cannot be washed away. The words we said, the mistakes of the past, the wrong decisions and indiscretions at times will not be washed away. Khalid ibn al-Walid (r.a.) could never go back and stop himself from what would be the death of Hamzah on the day of Uhud. He (r.a.) could never go back and undo the death of seventy of the *ṣaḥabah* in that holy ground of Uhud. He cannot undo it, but what he can do is hear Allah (s.w.t.) saying:

$$ ... إِنَّ ٱلْحَسَنَٰتِ يُذْهِبْنَ ٱلسَّيِّئَاتِ ۚ ... ﴿١١٤﴾ $$

Indeed, good deeds do away with misdeeds...

(Hud, 11:114)

Our righteous morality, our good deeds can wash away, can counterbalance, can offset and can extinguish the sins of our past. Allah (s.w.t.) further says near the end of *surah* al-Furqan:

$$ إِلَّا مَن تَابَ وَءَامَنَ وَعَمِلَ عَمَلًا صَٰلِحًا فَأُو۟لَٰٓئِكَ يُبَدِّلُ ٱللَّهُ سَيِّئَاتِهِمْ حَسَنَٰتٍ ۗ وَكَانَ ٱللَّهُ غَفُورًا رَّحِيمًا ﴿٧٠﴾ $$

Except for those who repent, believe and do righteous work. For them Allah will replace their evil deeds with good. And ever is Allah Forgiving and Merciful.

(al-Furqan, 25:70)

Allah says that those who repent, come back and do good instead of evil—they renew their faith and begin to practise good deeds, Allah will then transfer their sins to good deeds.

'Abdullah ibn Mas'ud (r.a.) mentions that there are two understandings of this—that our physical sin will become a good deed, and the burden will become heavy in your scale of good deed. The more preferred answer is that Allah will give us a long and good enough life and opportunity to earn good deeds that can counter the mistakes of our past. The Prophet (s.a.w.) further mentions that a person is left walking on the Earth until he is left without any sins:

It was narrated from Mus'ab bin Sa'd that his father, Sa'd bin Abu Waqqas, said:

"I said: 'O' Messenger of Allah, which people are most severely tested?' He said: 'The Prophets, then the next best and the next best. A person is tested according to his religious commitment. If he is steadfast in his religious commitment, he will be tested more severely, and if he is frail in his religious commitment, his test will be according to his commitment. Trials will continue to afflict a person until they leave him walking on the earth with no sin on him.'"

(Sunan ibn Majah 4023)

They are left walking on Earth so that they can commit to the commitment of intentionally going out of their way to seek and ask Allah for forgiveness, to do something momentous, and spend their energy and wealth in order to make that change of being without sin.

8. A humiliating consequence following behind you (ذنب)

Dhanab is a humiliating consequence that follows us and haunts us. I remember my father telling me, "Yahya, people humiliate themselves. They are not humiliated by others."

I never understood this when I was young. This is now something that I have been teaching my own children as well. I tell them "don't humiliate yourself and what I mean is don't do something that will cause someone to react in a way that will be humiliating to you." The Prophet (s.a.w.) talks about this matter in a simple way:

The Messenger of Allah said: "It is among the greatest of sins that a man should curse his parents." They said: "O' Messenger of Allah! Does a man curse his parents?" He said: "Yes. He verbally abuses the father of a man, who in turn, verbally abuses his father, and he (retaliates and) curses his mother, so he curses his mother."

(Jami' at-Tirmidhi 1902)

The Prophet (s.a.w.) says it in a simpler way. He (s.a.w.) said that the cursed is the man who curses his father—that they use vulgar language towards their father. The people wondered how such a thing could happen. The Prophet (s.a.w.) explains that it is because the person cursed the other man's father first. The other person started it first and the one receiving the vulgar language in return, as a natural response does the same thing.

So, basically who is the one who cursed their father to begin with? It is us. We do this to ourselves. The *dhanb*, humiliation that we bring upon ourselves, that we carry at times, is the consequence of our mistaken choices, our errors in judgement, our unwillingness to bring ourselves back from the brink. Allah (s.w.t.) warns us of having this mentality of "I say what I want to say and I do not care about the consequence." Have you heard people saying "I don't care what people think. They can't judge me. Only Allah can judge me." Unfortunately, this mentality is prevalent even amongst the Muslims and it is a completely unislamic concept. And so, people start to say that only Allah can judge them however when they are in the court for doing something wrong, they do not say that. The Prophet (s.a.w.) said in a hadith that we are all just Allah's witnesses on this Earth:

> A funeral procession passed and the people praised the deceased. The Prophet (s.a.w.) said, "It has been affirmed to him." Then another funeral procession passed and the people spoke badly of the deceased. The Prophet (s.a.w.) said, "It has been affirmed to him". 'Umar bin Al-Khaṭṭab asked (Allah's Messenger (s.a.w.), "What has been affirmed?" He replied, "You praised this, so Paradise has been affirmed to him; and you spoke badly of this, so Hell has been affirmed to him. You people are Allah's witnesses on earth."
>
> (Ṣaḥiḥ al-Bukhari 1367)

The Prophet (s.a.w.) said that if forty righteous people come and stand in our *janazah* and in their hearts they testify that the person is worthy of *Jannah*—they are then from the people of *Jannah*. However, for some of us, me for example, we do not necessarily need forty people. We just need our wife.

The Prophet (s.a.w.) further mentioned that we leave this world in one of these two ways—*al-mustarih* or *al-mustaraah minhu*. It is either we find comfort because we have left this life and Allah has given us comfort or the world is comforted by our departure. Allah said we are the witnesses.

Have you ever been to a *janazah* whereby the people who are there, praying in the *janazah*, are there because they are obliged and not because they want to. They are there not because they would move mountains to be there to make *ṣalah* for the *janazah*. And there are some people whom when we look we say "*SubḥanAllāh*"; these are the ones who don't know Allah, they are the ones who are asking Allah for the person who has passed away

Our end is defined by our life. It is defined by the ones who we sit and institute life with, by what we bring upon ourself, by what we define the scope of our life is—by what is left behind from our legacy, from our words, from our behaviours, from our demeanour, from our habits. what mourning does our spouse have for us and what do our children feel in aggrievement other than just emotion. What usefulness extends beyond us is determined by what opposes our self-humiliation and indignation.

Umar ibn al-Khaṭṭab (r.a.) had said this powerful statement, "We were the most humiliated people on earth and Allah gave us honour through Islam. If we ever seek honour through anything else, Allah will humiliate us again." It is a statement often mentioned and remembered. He (r.a.) is saying that we were all humiliated people until Allah ennobled us and honoured us with the Qur'an. And so, if we seek ascendancy, honour, nobility in other than the Qur'an, in contradiction to the Qur'an—Allah will then humiliate us and bring us down.

Therefore, the concept of what is *dhanb* is around— what we blame ourselves for, what we consider against ourselves, when or where we feel humiliation and whether we shy away from humiliation. Sometimes we feel humiliated from the things that should be praiseworthy. Sometimes we are shy to do the things that we are asked to do. Or sometimes we want people to know that deep down we are generous and giving. All these actions will be witnessed by people and they are the ones who will then be there at our *janazah*. Thus, it is important to know our mindset in how we view people and witness people as in this life and the thereafter it.

9. Mark (خطأ)

Khat in the Arabic language means a line or a mark.

Khat is a line. *Khata* is where we go and pass the mark, where we have gone beyond a limit that should have been a boundary. For example, those who play sports such as the long jump, will immediately fail if stepped out of line. The people would just say sorry and that is the end. Nothing can be done anymore. There is no further discussion because the line was already crossed when it shouldn't have been.

Khat, the line is not drawn by us but by Allah. Allah is the *shari'ah*, the lawgiver, the one who established the limitations of life. When we consider the enormity of crossing a line that is decided for us by Allah intentionally, it is different than if we did it unknowingly. For example, in the Olympic for the hundred-yard challenge, someone perhaps accidentally ran before the shot. Due to that, everyone will be asked to gather again so that they can retry, and restart the match. The person had crossed the mark, he went ahead when he was not supposed to. It was a mistake and thus was forgiven. However, the thing is, if we do it once (the crossing of boundaries and limits), we will only be forgiven the first time. When we keep repeating it, it becomes *lamam*, a compilation.

If we do not learn from the mistake, we end up doing

it more often and it then becomes a *lamam*. Eventually, the mistakes become a reality of one's life, reality, mindset, behaviour and intent. Allah asks us to make this *du'a'* to ask Him to not hold us accountable for the things that were genuine mistakes.:

$$ ... رَبَّنَا لَا تُؤَاخِذْنَآ إِن نَّسِينَآ أَوْ أَخْطَأْنَا ۚ ... ﴿٢٨٦﴾ $$

...Our Lord, do not impose blame upon us if we have forgotten or erred...

(al-Baqarah, 2:286)

Allah is *al-Ghafūr*. Allah will cast aside our mistakes when we make *du'a'* and repent to him. He forgives the mistakes that were not intentional, that was a slip; *zalah*. However, the sin which becomes premeditated and intentional becomes a *sayyiah* that we should be shameful for.

10. Shame (سيئة)

The Prophet (s.a.w.) said, "One of the sayings of the prophets which the people have got, is. 'If you do not feel ashamed, then do whatever you like."

(Ṣaḥiḥ al-Bukhari 3483)

When we feel no shame, it will cause us to do anything we want. We live in a world today where immorality has become deceptively aligned with personal liberty, unfortunately. As Muslims, we believe that there are absolute rights and wrongs. There are certain things that are right and wrong. There are certain things that are halal and certain things that are haram.

What is trying to be sold to us currently is the thought of believing that there are things which are **better and worse**. That if we were to do this, it is good, and if we were to do something else it will worsen our situation.

A paradigm shift from right and wrong, to better and worse. People want to move away from the right and wrong concept because the moment when there is something which is right and wrong beyond the understanding of human objective and subjective, it becomes the moment where we have to believe in the oversight of Allah, the lawgiver.

There is right and there is wrong.

There is *ḥasanah* and there is *sayyiah*.

There is good and there is evil.

There is moral and there is immorality—which is not just defined by what people in a particular time in human history believe is moral. If we were to look over the prophecies that the Prophet (s.a.w.) mentioned, we can see that some of them are extremely striking as we can see it today. For instance, on personal freedoms, people living however they want and desire, homosexuality and lesbianism, illegal sexual intercourse, the drinking of alcohol, etc.

In human history, there have been many moments of what we believe immoral sexual deviancy. It was categorised in all of its different ways but never in human history was it government sanctioned—that the immoral sexual deviancy act is allowed, there is a contract, and it is enshrined in law. That has never happened in all of human history—not even during the Romans and the Greeks' time.

Therefore, the *sayyiah*, the deed and its categorisation of it are important to know and realise right and wrong in it. It is important for us to know right and wrong when we live in a context where something is seen as permissible, acceptable, adapted, adopted, enabled, and preferred—even though it is known to us that within our tradition, revelation, religion that what remains is our value to judge the right from wrong, the halal from haram and not by better and worse.

11. Public Oppression (بغي)

Baghi is where a person is oppressive and he does it publicly because they believe none can hold them accountable. We live in a time where *baghi* is where the one who is bombing is seen as the victim. Can you imagine? A Scottish journalist mentioned the world mourns for innocent citizens of Ukraine who were fired with the Russian rockets in a span of a month. However, nobody mourned for the people of Gaza who were also fired at in a span of an hour.

Fir'awn on the other hand also did *baghi*. When the magician prostrated to Allah after witnessing the miracle through Musa (a.s.), Fir'awn said "I'm going to crucify you and hang you up in the stocks of these date trees, the highest public place we have in the centre of town." That he was going to publicly punish the people and oppress them if they turn to Allah.

… فَلَأُقَطِّعَنَّ أَيْدِيَكُمْ وَأَرْجُلَكُم مِّنْ خِلَـٰفٍ وَلَأُصَلِّبَنَّكُمْ فِى جُذُوعِ ٱلنَّخْلِ وَلَتَعْلَمُنَّ أَيُّنَآ أَشَدُّ عَذَابًا وَأَبْقَىٰ ﴿٧١﴾

…So I will surely cut off your hands and your feet on opposite sides, and I will crucify you on the trunks of palm trees, and you will surely know which of us is more severe in [giving] punishment and more enduring."

(Ṭaha, 20:71)

Firʿawn is basically trying to prove and show who is the one who is more severe in punishment, him or Allah, the God of Musa.

The problem with *baghi* is that it becomes the tipping point to Allah's punishment. The moment our oppression to another becomes public and we do not hold ourselves back—then we have to find shelter for the punishment of Allah is imminent. And that becomes a consistent warning to individuals and collectives. May the might of Allah (s.w.t.) show its presence so that we feel the vindication of those who have been dishonoured by the *baghi* of the oppressors.

12. Breaks promise (حنث)

The breaking of promises is one of those statements that Allah (s.w.t.) warns us about as being a precursor to action. As we become liberal with our heart, its first effect is shown through our tongue and its ongoing effect is shown in our demonstrated behaviour into the actions of our body—into the mechanisms that we now enact on account of it.

Before Fir'awn began oppressing and seeking to punish the people of Bani Isra'il and Musa (a.s.), his sin was more about the lies that he spoke. And so, Musa comes and say:

$$\text{أَنْ أَرْسِلْ مَعَنَا بَنِيٓ إِسْرَٰٓءِيلَ ۝}$$

[Commanded to say], "Send with us the Children of Israel."

(ash-Shu'ara', 26:17)

He tells Fir'awn to let the people of Bani Isra'il go. They all want to leave the land and do not want to stay. They do not want anything from him and to keep everything as it is if he does not want to accept the truth. Fir'awn then turns to his people and says:

$$\text{يُرِيدُ أَن يُخْرِجَكُم مِّنْ أَرْضِكُم بِسِحْرِهِۦ فَمَاذَا تَأْمُرُونَ ۝}$$

He wants to drive you out of your land by his magic, so what do you advise?"

(ash-Shu'ara', 26:35)

Fir'awn, instead, told the people that Musa wants to

take the land when he actually said that he wanted to leave the land. That he and the Children of Israel want to cross the sea and not be with him.

Ḥinth, the breaking of statement. The dishonesty that is spoken is one of the capital crimes that is registered with us in the Qur'an.

13. Evil Conduct (سوء العمل)

The breaking of promises, the breaking of our statements, and the incompleteness of our words leads to *su'ul 'amal*, the evil conduct. *Su'ul 'amal* is the action that is performed which is considered evil and unacceptable. That the deeds should not be performed in this manner as it is wrong.

Normally with *'amal* there are two sides to the same coin. A person can do the same deed in that which is halal and earn reward or do the same deed in that which is haram and let it become their enigmatic and sin before Allah. Any *'amal* that we envision and take upon ourselves can have one of these two courses. The *'amal* can be something that we are choosing to do that will be pleasing to Allah even if the *'amal* is outwardly righteous. For instance, *salah*. If we do our *salah* in the proper manner and solely for Allah, we will earn Allah's rewards. The other course or the other side of the coin could be that the *salah*, the *niyyah* (intention) of the *salah* is not for Allah—as mentioned by our Prophet (s.a.w.) of his fear for his *ummah* who will be committing the minor *shirk* of worshipping Allah because of others eye that has fallen upon them. Suddenly, the *'amal* that was meant to be whole and complete, and for Allah becomes something that is of a discrepancy and a disgrace for the individual. The collection of sinful deeds leads a person to become callous and enter into *ma'siyat*.

14. Opposing command (عصى)

Ma'siyat comes from the word *'asa*. As mentioned, the collection of sinful deeds leads a person to become callous and enter into *ma'siyat*. In the Arabic language, when people speak about driftwood, stick or branch they use the word *'asa*. The reason for this is mentioned in the Qur'an:

$$\text{قَالَ هِيَ عَصَايَ أَتَوَكَّؤُاْ عَلَيْهَا وَأَهُشُّ بِهَا عَلَىٰ غَنَمِي وَلِيَ فِيهَا مَآرِبُ أُخْرَىٰ ﴿١٨﴾}$$

He said, "It is my staff; I lean upon it, and I bring down leaves for my sheep and I have therein other uses."

(Ṭaha, 20:18)

Allah asks Musa what he is holding and his response was

that it is his staff, *ʿasa.* Sayyidina ʿUmar also had a famous statement where he mentioned *ʿasa,* stick. He said that the stick will be used to the one who does what deserves to be beaten by the stick.

ʿAsa is for the one who does the *maʿsiyat.* What is the concept of *ʿasa*? Why is it referred to as a stick? When we do good deeds, we are living, we are nurturing ourselves and others as well. The picture of a believer is that of a fruitful tree as the Prophet (s.a.w.) described. And so, when we are doing what is expected to our family, relatives, workplace, home—we become a tree whose roots are deep, whose trunk is solid, and whose branches extend and overhang. Thus, providing shade, shelter and fruit to not just ourselves, but to anyone who is in our vicinity. The hypocrite is the one who Allah describes in the Qur'an as being like a hollowed piece of timber:

وَإِذَا رَأَيْتَهُمْ تُعْجِبُكَ أَجْسَامُهُمْ ۖ وَإِن يَقُولُوا تَسْمَعْ لِقَوْلِهِمْ ۖ كَأَنَّهُمْ خُشُبٌ مُّسَنَّدَةٌ ۖ يَحْسَبُونَ كُلَّ صَيْحَةٍ عَلَيْهِمْ ۚ هُمُ الْعَدُوُّ فَاحْذَرْهُمْ ۚ قَاتَلَهُمُ اللَّهُ ۖ أَنَّىٰ يُؤْفَكُونَ ﴿٤﴾

And when you see them, their forms please you, and if they speak, you listen to their speech. [They are] as if they were pieces of wood propped up - they think that every shout is against them. They are the enemy, so beware of them. May Allah destroy them; how are they deluded?

(al-Munafiqun, 63:4)

The hypocrites are like a tree that has been cut down and is now just a piece of wood but the wood is dead. It is worthy of nothing except to be burned to provide warmth or to be leaned on. It has nothing that it can offer of itself anymore. It's only consumption is to be consumed and put away—it is driftwood. When we build our life consistently on *ma'siyat,* we become a fungus and cancer to the tree of our life. Each and every *ma'siyat* weakens our soils and our roots; it kills off our fruits and our leaves until we become a hallowed piece of timber that can be easily cast aside and thrown to be consumed by the fire.

Therefore, the concept of *'asa* is that we change our living state into death. We become as described earlier the walking dead—the ones who are eating, drinking and enjoying but don't have the heart which has faith that gives them the life with Allah. And so, Allah (s.w.t.) tells us in the Qur'an that the worst type of human beings are the ones who eat, drink, enjoy and have merriment in their life, but then Hellfire becomes their destitute. Allah says:

وَلَقَدْ ذَرَأْنَا لِجَهَنَّمَ كَثِيرًا مِّنَ ٱلْجِنِّ وَٱلْإِنسِ ۖ لَهُمْ قُلُوبٌ لَّا يَفْقَهُونَ بِهَا وَلَهُمْ أَعْيُنٌ لَّا يُبْصِرُونَ بِهَا وَلَهُمْ ءَاذَانٌ لَّا يَسْمَعُونَ بِهَآ ۚ أُو۟لَـٰٓئِكَ كَٱلْأَنْعَـٰمِ بَلْ هُمْ أَضَلُّ ۚ أُو۟لَـٰٓئِكَ هُمُ ٱلْغَـٰفِلُونَ ﴿١٧٩﴾

And We have certainly created for Hell many of the jinn and mankind. They have hearts with which they do not understand, they have eyes with which they do not see, and they have ears with which they do not hear. Those are like livestock; rather, they are more astray. It is they who are the heedless.

(al-A'raf, 7:179)

They have eyes but they do not see with it.

They can look with it, but they do not see the truth.

They have ears that hear but they cannot listen to the truth.

They have hearts that beat but they do not perceive the reality of the truth.

They are nothing more than cattle. In fact, they are worse. There are those who are distracted by the next life as they find this life of greater value.

15. Public indecency, & obscenity (فاحشة) & Wrong oneself (ظلمنا نفسه)

Faḥishah in relative terms is a major sin. *Faḥishah* is related to public sexual immorality or we are going against the command of Allah publicly—acknowledging a sin publicly and in front of others. Allah (s.w.t.) describes a moment of public indecency which happened amongst the *ṣaḥabah* and the incident the following incident is where Allah reveals one of the verses that combine the two sins—public indecency and obscenity, and the sin of wronging oneself (the *ẓulm* a person commits on him/herself)

The incident occurred during the Battle of Uhud. A year before the battle, the Prophet (s.a.w.) was victorious in the Battle of Badr as Allah (s.w.t.) sent angels to fight along with him and the *ṣaḥabah*. 313 righteous souls brought about the defeat of an army that was far from their capacity. During the Battle of Badr, the righteous Muslims only had two armoured horses in their army while the Quraysh had 200 mounted knights. Imagine the scene of the battle. Despite the Quraysh having more possibility of winning,

Allah instead delivered victory to the Prophet (s.a.w.). After the defeat, the people of Quraysh, the *mushrikun*, wanted to reclaim their honour as well as their superior stance amongst the Arab tribes as they did not want to be looked down upon. And so, for the Battle of Uhud, the Quraysh had an army of 3 000 people. They brought their women to the battle as well to encourage them to feel shameful if they were to flee from the battle. When the Prophet (s.a.w.) heard of their advance and number of army, he (s.a.w.) decided on a strategic plan; to be at a strategic location near the mountain of Uhud.

I want to briefly explain the background of *Madinat an-Nabi*, the city of the Prophet (s.a.w.). One of the miracles of Yathrib or now known as *Madinah Al Munawwarah* (The Enlightened City), it was a city that was just off the path of the caravans that would go from Yemen into Transjordan and Sham. The city held such strategic value and arable land where people cultivated fruits and dates as well. It was a city that was just off the path enough that people did not conquer it and just thought of it as worth visiting. Yathrib was also a city that was defended by mountains of lava whereby three sides of it have massive lava flows. Furthermore, Yathrib also has, under it, flowing rivers of fresh water unlike other places in Arabia, hence that is why Madinah had seven wells while Makkah only had two.

The people of Yathrib are Yemeni, unlike the other Arab tribes who were usually Qahtan, Najdi and so on. By nature, the Yemenis were very fierce warriors. They were people who came from the area of the great dam of Ma'rib. Ma'rib Dam was one of those archaeological astounding wonders of the world, and it was destroyed by a flood that forced its people to migrate up. They found arable land, Yathrib, that was similar to what they had in Yemen and so they settled themselves. They are the people of Bani Aws and Bani Khazraj. The people there were accepting of having more than one faith. There were Jews, Christians, idolaters, etc. The place consisted of a unique category of Arab people. The Prophet (s.a.w.) lived amongst them and at the very end of Madinah, at the back at Khaybar, were the people of the Jewish tribes called Bani Qaynuqa, Bani Nadir, Bani Qurayza. The people were near where the lava was flowing. It is where the Prophet (s.a.w.) had signed a peace treaty that the people would cover his flank. This is where Allah tells the Prophet (s.a.w.), especially during the Battle of Khandak to not take the Jews and Christians as absolute protectors:

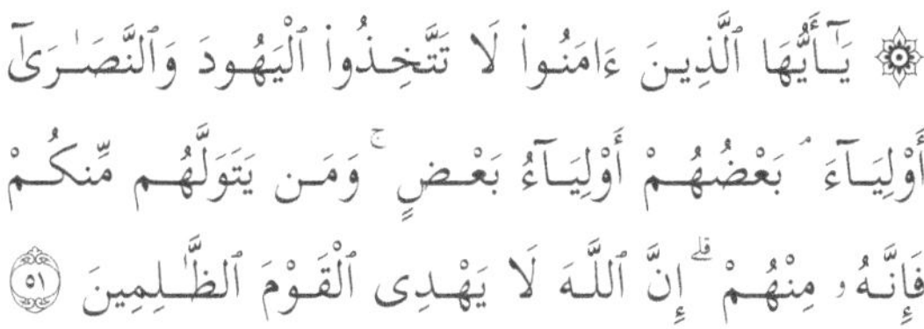

O' you who have believed, do not take the Jews and the Christians as allies. They are [in fact] allies of one another. And whoever is an ally to them among you—then indeed, he is [one] of them. Indeed, Allah guides not the wrongdoing people.

(al-Ma'idah, 5:51)

And so back to the Battle of Uhud. The area of Yathrib is strategic, it is covered with lava fields. Near the mountain of Uhud, *Jabal al-Rumah* or also known as *Jabal Ainain* is where the Prophet (s.a.w.) strategically positioned the Muslim archers. The Prophet (s.a.w.) chose the fifty archers to be at the top of that mountain and told them to not leave the place no matter what happens—that even if the birds in heaven were to come down and snatch them off the ground, they were still not allowed to leave the place:

Narrated Al-Bara bin Azib:

The Prophet (s.a.w.) appointed `Abdullah bin Jubair as the commander of the infantry men (archers) who were fifty on the day (of the battle) of Uḥud. He instructed them, "Stick to your place, and don't leave it even if you see birds snatching us, till I send for you; and if you see that we have defeated the infidels and made them flee, even then you should not leave your place till I send for you." Then the infidels were defeated. By Allah, I saw the women fleeing lifting up their clothes revealing their leg-bangles and their legs. So, the companions of 'Abdullah bin Jubair said, "The booty! O' people, the booty! Your companions have become victorious, what are you waiting for now?" 'Abdullah bin Jubair said, "Have you forgotten what Allah's Messenger (s.a.w.) said to you?" They replied, "By Allah! We will go to the people (i.e. the enemy) and collect our share from the war booty." But when they went to them, they were forced to turn back defeated. At that time Allah's Messenger (s.a.w.) in their rear was calling them back. Only twelve men remained with the Prophet (s.a.w.) and the infidels martyred seventy men from us…

(Ṣaḥīḥ al-Bukhari 3039)

The Prophet asked the archers to pledge and they all did. Then the Prophet (s.a.w.) aligned his camp. He then was at the forefront of the battle. A note here that I would like everyone to take is to remember and realise that our Prophet (s.a.w.) was not a coward. He (s.a.w.) was a person who owned swords. It was not just one or two swords but eleven swords. Some *riwayat* even say thirteen swords. He (s.a.w.) was a person who was ready at any moment of notice to defend the truth, right until his death. ʿAli (r.a.) mentioned in a hadith that whenever the battle started to get fierce, he and the people would hide and seek shelter by being behind the Prophet (s.a.w.):

It was narrated that ʿAli (r.a.) said:

When the fighting intensified and the two sides met in battle, we sought shelter with the Messenger of Allah (s.a.w.) and no one was closer to the enemy than him.

(Musnad Aḥmad 1347)

I want to highlight here that ʿAli (r.a.) was not an ordinary man and for him to say that he would take shelter behind the Prophet (s.a.w.) means a huge deal. ʿAli (r.a.) was that man whom the Prophet (s.a.w.) sent to the people of Bahrain to collect the *zakat*. He (r.a.) went out alone on foot from Madinah to Bahrain. As he was walking towards his destination, some of the tribes who were aligned with the Quraysh saw him and identified him as the Prophet (s.a.w.)'s son-in-law. They planned to hold him for ransom as they thought they could get a lot of gold from the Prophet (s.a.w.), even more than the Quraysh. However, one of the people said "But that is 'Ali. He is no ordinary person." And so they suggested among themselves to send 100 men to capture 'Ali. However, some still felt reluctant. They then came to the conclusion of sending 200 men just to capture one man. They galloped and went to 'Ali and said "give yourself up peacefully." 'Ali (r.a.) was confused and he did not want to fight or hurt anyone. However, they continued with their wants as they felt confident with their number. 'Ali (r.a.) was quick on his feet and thought of a plan. He strategically led the people up a small hill. 100 men followed 'Ali (r.a.) up the hill and afterwards they never came down. None returned. The remaining 100 men were confused. They were contemplating whether or not they should go up the hill or retreat but then they imagined the questions they would be asked by the woman in regard to where their husband and son were. And so, they decided to make another attempt to capture 'Ali as they did not want to be humiliated. The 100 remaining people went up and only twenty remained. 'Ali (r.a.) took twenty of them as captives.

And so, when this brave man, 'Ali (r.a.) says that when he is scared he hides behind the Prophet (s.a.w.), it just goes to show how brave the Prophet (s.a.w.) is. At the Battle of Uhud, the Muslims are pushing forwards and the people on the hill see a light of success. They reminisce about the Battle of Badr and think that Allah will send down angels once more to save his beloved Prophet Muḥammad (s.a.w.). The people at the hill were attracted by the horses and bounty of the battle that was left stranded. Bounty was a part of the treasure of the war and was allowed in the *deen* that it can be taken. And so, the *dunya* attracted the people on the hill as they left their position to grab the spoils of war which then caused a lot of deaths of the Muslims. They left their positions at the hill, and the flank became vulnerable. Some of the noblest of the *ṣaḥabah* of the Prophet (s.a.w.) were killed. According to a few *riwayat*, there were either three to five people who remained. The act of the Muslims coming down the hill, disobeying the messenger of Allah— became a *faḥishah* as they publically did the opposite of what they were ordered to do. At least seventy of the *ṣaḥabah* were martyred; Ḥamzah ibn ʿAbdul Muṭalib (r.a.), Muṣʿab ibn ʿUmayr (r.a.), ʿAmr ibn al-Jamuḥ (r.a.), Abu Dahda (r.a.), Julaybib (r.a.), Anas ibn Naḍr (r.a.), etc. The Prophet (s.a.w.) also as a consequence was hurt. Umm ʿUmara or also known as Nusaybah bint Kaʿab was covering and defending the Prophet (s.a.w.) despite her whole body being wounded. The Muslims retreated. They were defeated. As the night fell, the *mushrikun* began to party and drink in their revelry, abuse and desecration of the bodies of the *ṣaḥabah*.

I want you to imagine yourself being amongst the disobedient ones who came down the hill, who disobeyed the messenger of Allah (s.w.t.). You are seated at that moment in the dark, and you realise due to your disobedience, Hamzah (r.a.) is in *Jannah* but he is also no longer present in the Prophet (s.a.w.)'s life. You are seated amongst the Prophet (s.a.w.) and are looking at his blessed face that was injured due to your actions of choosing the *dunya* over the *akhirah*; and you know at any time, Jibril will descend with words of revelation regarding what happened and what is to happen. Imagine the shame of your *sayyiah*. Imagine that moment of fear. Imagine what you consider to be a sin that will lead you away from *Jannah*. And then Allah says:

۞ وَسَارِعُوٓا۟ إِلَىٰ مَغْفِرَةٍ مِّن رَّبِّكُمْ وَجَنَّةٍ عَرْضُهَا ٱلسَّمَـٰوَٰتُ وَٱلْأَرْضُ أُعِدَّتْ لِلْمُتَّقِينَ ۝١٣٣ ٱلَّذِينَ يُنفِقُونَ فِى ٱلسَّرَّآءِ وَٱلضَّرَّآءِ وَٱلْكَـٰظِمِينَ ٱلْغَيْظَ وَٱلْعَافِينَ عَنِ ٱلنَّاسِ ۗ وَٱللَّهُ يُحِبُّ ٱلْمُحْسِنِينَ ۝١٣٤ وَٱلَّذِينَ إِذَا فَعَلُوا۟ فَـٰحِشَةً أَوْ ظَلَمُوٓا۟ أَنفُسَهُمْ ذَكَرُوا۟ ٱللَّهَ فَٱسْتَغْفَرُوا۟ لِذُنُوبِهِمْ وَمَن يَغْفِرُ ٱلذُّنُوبَ إِلَّا ٱللَّهُ وَلَمْ يُصِرُّوا۟ عَلَىٰ مَا فَعَلُوا۟ وَهُمْ يَعْلَمُونَ ۝١٣٥

And hasten to forgiveness from your Lord and a garden [i.e., Paradise] as wide as the heavens and earth, prepared for the righteous.Who spend [in the cause of Allah] during ease and hardship and who restrain anger and who pardon the people—and Allah loves the doers of good;And those who, when they commit an immorality or wrong themselves [by transgression], remember Allah and seek forgiveness for their sins—and who can forgive sins except Allah?—and [who] do not persist in what they have done while they know.

(Ali-ʿImran, 3:133-135)

Allah is saying to hurry, to race one another to His forgiveness and the heavens that awaits them—for those who have *taqwa* (piety). *SubhanAllāh*. The *Jannah* is for those who return back to Allah; those who when they commit *fahishah* or wrong themselves and then they return through the remembrance of Allah and by seeking His forgiveness. *SubhanAllāh*. Who can forgive them more or in better than Allah (s.w.t.).

Dear brothers and sisters, there is nothing that we will do which will exceed that moment. There is no crime that we will commit which will put us further away from *Jannah* than what the *sahabah* and Muslims had thought of themselves at that moment. There is no place where we are going to wonder, "I have lost *Jannah*", "What hope do I have now?", "What place will there be in *Jannah* for me?", "I am the reason that this happened"," I caused this to myself", like the people who disobeyed. Instead, Allah says to race to *Jannah*. Allah says *Jannah* is for those who remember Him after a mistake; for those who do not want to repeat their error; for those who understand that Allah's mercy is vast and their commitment to correction is their saving grace.

Allah often uses these two words in combination—*faḥishah* and *ẓalamu anfusahum*—often in the Qur'an. Both the sins of doing wrong publicly or privately should not be seen as one in favour or worse than the others. Unfortunately, in our human capacity, we calculate that our private sins are hidden as nobody knows and because Allah hides them as He is *As-Sittīr*, the one who hides our sins. However, our private and personal sins is not a sin that is lesser even if many people do not know because if we were to think that, that means we are more fearful of people than Allah (s.w.t.). One of the terrifying hadith of the Prophet (s.a.w.) is that he mentions of those who on the Day of Judgement when they open their book of good deeds, all their good deeds (prayer, fasting, *ḥajj*,) will scatter away like dust. It will then be said to those people to catch their good deeds. Those people will ask "O'Allah why is this happening to us?", "Why are all our good deeds going away?" It will be said that it is due to the fact that we relished in our private sins and did our best to cover our public. It is because we were more concerned about the public condemnation than what was in Allah's sight of your conditions and circumstances:

> "I certainly know people of my nation who will come on the Day of Resurrection with good deeds like the mountains of Tihamah, but Allah will make them like scattered dust." Thawban said: "O' Messenger of Allah, describe them to us and tell us more, so that we will not become of them unknowingly." He said: "They are your brothers and from your race, worshipping at night as you do, but they will be people who, when they are alone, transgress the sacred limits of Allah."
>
> (Sunan ibn Majah 4245)

16. Darkness & Oppression (ظلم)

Darkness, *zulma* is synonymous in the Arabic language with oppression. *Zulm* in the syntax of the Qur'an is the opposite of wisdom. When we ask somebody to do something they are incapable of, it means we are oppressing them.

Let me give you an example. If I were to ask someone who does not have any knowledge in the Arabic language, to write me a letter in the Arabic language—means that I am asking them to do something that they are unequipped to do. I am the one who is wrong, not the other party for not being able to do it. Therefore, we can evidently see oppression in a relationship, power struggle, finance, government, business, and more: We can see that there is an element whereby somebody is tasked with something they are incapable of providing and doing.

Wisdom, the opposite of *zulm*, on the other hand, means that we are putting everything into its right place. We are giving everyone and everything the right amount of time; the right measure to do things in the right space, time and ability they are required to do.

For this reason, when we are speaking about oppression, we are also speaking about darkness. This is because when someone is incapable of doing something they do not know, they will feel down. They feel that they are held under and left out in the dark. We definitely have someone around us, who perhaps is in a business and they are feeling down. They might say " I was left out in the dark. I don't know what to do. I wasn't told about this. I wasn't aware. It's not my fault." This happens due to oppression.

In addition, there is no greater *zulm* than to worship

other than Allah.

$$\dots\ \text{إِنَّ ٱلشِّرْكَ لَظُلْمٌ عَظِيمٌ}\ \text{(١٣)}$$

..Indeed, association [with Him] is great injustice."

(Luqman, 31:13)

Why is *shirk* such a great oppression? This is because we are asking other than Allah to do something for us. For instance, worshiping and asking the idol to do something that it is incapable of doing. And so, it is not just wrong, but it is also oppression as we are asking something to do what they cannot do—even if it is the Prophet (s.a.w.). We are wronging ourselves and others. Hence, *zulm* also becomes one of the reasons why people commit fasiq.

17. Crossing the boundaries (فسق)

When we are feeling unsupported, unloved, held under, not knowing what to do, not being able to make up for something despite apologising many times—despite trying to make amends and put in more effort, but to no avail, *fisq* is being bred. Those feelings breeds *fisq* or also known as *fasiq*.

Fisq gives people greater access to darkness than they should have. It does not mean that it legitimises it, but it explains it. Hence, sometimes when a person feels that they are wronged, unmet, and devalued—they then act in a way that pushes them further away from the truth and part of it, the blame at times is upon those who were not supportive to their process.

In Australia, there is a programme called "Are You OK?" It is an Australian initiative to ask people whether they are fine. The Prophet (s.a.w.) was that kind of a man, who frequently asked people whether they were alright. The Prophet (s.a.w.) was caring to everyone as well including children. The Prophet (s.a.w.) even comforted a child who had lost his pet bird. Anas ibn Malik had a younger brother who went by the nickname Abu 'Umayr and he had a sparrow. The sparrow (*al-nughayr*) had a cage and Abu 'Umayr would feed it. He loved the sparrow, his pet but one day it died. When the Prophet (s.a.w.) heard from Anas about the death of the bird, he (s.a.w.) said to the *sahabah that* "Let's visit him." And so, the Prophet (s.a.w.) comforted the young child for the loss of his bird.

> Anas b. Malik said : The Messenger of Allah (May peace be upon him) used to come to visit us. I had a younger brother who was called Abu 'Umair by Kunyah (surname). He had a sparrow with which he played, but it died. So one day the prophet

(May peace be upon him) came to see him and saw him grieved. He asked: What is the matter with him? The people replied: His sparrow has died. He then said: Abu 'Umair! What has happened to the little sparrow?

(Sunan Abi Dawud 4969)

Look at how the Prophet (s.a.w.) was with people and reflect. Look at ourselves and think about how we interact and behave with people.

Once, there was a woman who had a problem with her *mukh* (brain). The *ṣaḥabah* mentioned that it is because she had a brain injury. The woman was a rambler who would just stand and talk to herself. One day, the Prophet (s.a.w.) went out of his house and the woman can in front of him. She wanted to talk about one thing to the Prophet (s.a.w.). She was blocking the way as she stood in the middle of the road. Thus, the Prophet said to her that "Let us move out from the path of people and talk about a lot of things instead of just one." And so, the Prophet (s.a.w.) stood with her and listened to her talk for a long time. The Prophet (s.a.w.) listened to her talk until she was content.

Sometimes we can become the reason for people to go a little bit further in life or on the contrary we can become the reason for a person's *zulm*. We can become the reason for thir feeling disregarded, unimportant and left in the dark with no hope. And so, we must understand that our behaviour can affect another person, hence we should make sure we are in moderation. It is not right for those affected by *zulm* to do further things or go further away, however, as mentioned it gives a reason that we can understand that our behaviour must also be moderated.

18. Opposition (خالف)

Khilaf, to oppose. Some people are just opposites. Some people say "No, but." When we tell them to turn right on the road to get to the destination, they would turn left instead. They are opposed to the truth. Devaluing the truth, opposing the truth and opposing those who uphold the truth is a major infraction of the heart.

19. Pressure (مقتًا)

Maqt, pressure. We live in a world where at times there is so much pressure. Releasing the pressure of another believer is actually one of the greatest acts of deed. There is an interesting hadith where it is called the story of the one who is forgiven of without good deeds. He is forgiven of his sins, without having any good deed. *SubḥanAllāh*. He had no good deeds like he had no *ṣalah* deeds.

Allah's Messenger (s.a.w.) said, "A man used to give loans to the people and used to say to his servant, 'If the debtor is poor, forgive him, so that Allah may forgive us.' So when he met Allah (after his death), Allah forgave him."

(Ṣaḥīḥ al-Bukhari 3480)

A man will be brought in front of Allah (s.w.t.) on the Day of Judgement. When his record of good deeds are opened, they angels will ask "Did you do any good? Because there is nothing here in your record." There is nothing, not even a single sentence. As he is infront of Allah, he says to Allah that the has nothing. Actually, the man was wealthy. He used to give loans to people. He would say to those who collected his loans that, if they seem like people who could pay him back then tell them "if you can pay, please pay but if you need more time, then take more time." On the other hand, if the people are in a dire situation, if they have nothing, then the man said to cancel their debt, that he would forgive them. The man mentioned that he used to do that to try and help people, that is all. And so, Allah (s.w.t.) says to this man that "You are not more generous than me. I forgive you everything." Look at the mercy of Allah (s.w.t.). *SubḥanAllāh.*

The man would forgive the one who is unable to give back. It did not matter whether the amount was large or small. He would forgive it. He would release the pressure and would not add the pressure unto others. Therefore, don't discount any good deed that can be a pathway to our *Jannah*. If someone is in need, help them, give them the help they need. If they cannot return it back, forgive them. Imam Nawawi mentioned that the reason why the man was given escape with the mercy of Allah is because:

> "Whoever relieves a Muslim of a burden from the burdens of the world, Allah will relieve him of a burden from the burdens on the Day of Judgement. And whoever helps ease a difficulty in the world, Allah will grant him ease from a difficulty in the world and in the Hereafter. And whoever covers (the faults of) a Muslim, Allah will cover (his faults) for him in the world and the Hereafter. And Allah is engaged in helping the worshipper as long as the worshipper is engaged in helping his brother."

> (Jami' at-Tirmidhi 1930)

The one who releases a burden upon a person in this *dunya*, Allah will release the burden in the *akhirah*.

Part 3:
How Do We
Achieve Purity?

Chapter 11:
A Psychology of Redemption and *Tawbah*

As we begin now to seek purity and seek with Allah a *tasfiyah* (purification)—a cleansing, a beginning—we begin to assume that Allah (s.w.t.) knows that our growth and destination of what we can be, where we can transmit, and what we transition ourselves into, is very much within our intention and action. And every time we seek purity, every time we seek something that is better than what we have established in our life, our life is enriched on account of it.

So I want to study the concept of *tuhr* (purify), *taharah* (purity), *tasfiyah* (purification), and *tazkiyyah* (sanctification), in whichever way you want to use it. The concept of adulteration; coming to cleansing, coming to purification, coming to making something whole that was divided into parts, all of those are imageries that are provided to us by Allah in the Qur'an. The presumption, of course, for us is that there will be moments in our lives when we become tarnished and marked. There will be moments in our lives when we disfigure ourselves, our conduct, and our behaviour. There will be moments in our lives when we find shame and grief from them, that we recognise this is not the best of us, and the Prophet (s.a.w.) used to say that warning often. He would say لَيْسَ مِنَّا which means they are not from us. It is a way of warning; "You're losing your path. You're walking off the *sirat*. You're straying away from the middle. You're losing yourself from the pack. You're going into a place that is an unrecognisable territory, and you're setting yourself up to be devoured by the wolves, the *shayṭan*, the inhibitions of your souls.

Zebras are a very interesting creature of Allah. How does a zebra look? Do they camouflage really well in the African Savannah? Do the white and black pattern blend well in the natural environment? How is that an adaptive behaviour to save them from being preyed on by the wolves, leopards and hyenas? Even though these zebras stand out in that black and white pattern of theirs, they actually are very good at camouflaging within each other. When they are together in one group, the wolves, the leopards, and even the lions, could not find their primary target as they are always shifting between one another. However, scientists decided to mark a zebra with a red dye using a pellet gun to identify their target, hence making that one zebra the first prey. It was the first one that made itself different from its *ummah*. It was the first one that went off on its own. And the Prophet (s.a.w.), would always tell us, فَسَدِّدُوا وَقَارِبُوا come in the middle, gather in the *masjid*, come for your *jama'ah*.

"Abu Ad-Darda said to me: 'Where do you live?' I said: 'In a town near Hims.' Abu Ad-Darda said: 'I heard the Messenger of Allah (s.a.w.) say: "There are no three people in a town or encampment among whom prayer is not established, but the *shaytan* takes control of them. Therefore, stick to the congregation, for the wolf eats the sheep that strays off on its own." (One of the narrators (As Sa'ib) said: "The congregation means the congregational prayer."

(Sunan an-Nasa'i 847)

It is the one who leaves the *jama'ah* that is attacked by the wolf first. It is the sheep that strays away from the flock that is set upon. And as that mindset begins to replenish itself, we think of purity. One of the first things ordered upon the Prophet (s.a.w.) was:

$$\text{يَـٰٓأَيُّهَا ٱلْمُزَّمِّلُ ۝ قُمِ ٱلَّيْلَ إِلَّا قَلِيلًا ۝}$$

O' you who wraps himself (in clothing). Arise (to pray) the night, except for a little-

(al-Muzammil, 73:1-2)

Allah said, *yā ayyuhal muzzammil*, "O' you who is cloaked and covered," terrified by this new message that has come to you, *qum*, "stand up." But instead of busying ourselves with others, it is, *qum illayl 'illa qalila*, "Stand up before Allah

119

individually, privately in the night except for a few hours."

The same moment is now described in another way in *surah* al-Muddaththir:

$$\text{يَـٰٓأَيُّهَا ٱلْمُدَّثِّرُ ۝ قُمْ فَأَنذِرْ ۝ وَرَبَّكَ فَكَبِّرْ ۝ وَثِيَابَكَ فَطَهِّرْ ۝ وَٱلرُّجْزَ فَٱهْجُرْ ۝}$$

O' you who covers himself (with garments). Arise and warn others. And glorify your Lord. And purify your cloth. And avoid uncleanliness.

(al-Muddaththir, 74:1-5)

In the first instance, *qum fa'andhir,* "standup and warn others," *wa thiābaka faṭahhir,* "cleanse your cloths." The language or the imagery of the Qur'an on *thiyab* (cloth) is not just about attire. It is about the clothing that we govern ourselves with, meaning the character that we show others. When people say "clothing makes the men," it is not just based on the fine-tailored suit, it means that the clothing that we wear is what other people see us with from a distance. It is how people recognise us, it is what people instantaneously think of when they hear our name or our description, or when we are brought up in a conversation. So Allah says to the prophet, *thiyābaka faṭahhir,* meaning to make sure that what people recognise us by is through the markings of our clothing, as it is where the regality of our behaviour is distinguished. *War rujza* (uncleanliness), and "discard all that impurity out of your life (s.a.w.), *ummah* of Muḥammad."

Purity and purification become the stepping stone to undoing the marking of sin. When the Prophet (s.a.w.) speaks about *ma'asi, zallah, khaṭa, khaṭiah, ithm,* and *maqt,* he (s.a.w.) speaks about their effect. He (s.a.w.) says that "never does a person commit an act that is reprehensible, except it places on their heart *nukta sauda'*(black dot)." It darkens their heart with a spot and blemish. And each and every spot that is added to the other, becomes an incrustation, a rustication, an oxidation of the heart.

> "When the believer commits sin, a black spot appears on his heart. If he repents and gives up that sin and seeks forgiveness, his heart will be polished. But if (the sin) increases, (the black spot) increases. That is the Ran that Allah mentions in His Book: 'Nay! But on their hearts is the Ran (covering of sins and evil deeds) which they used to earn.'" [83:14]
>
> (Sunan ibn Majah 4244)

Oxidation is rust; a metal-eating itself. Your heart starts becoming toxic to itself, you start self-harming to your own detriment into the future. Your centre where your soul resides, where your *nafs* exist can become impregnable, and light cannot enter upon it. It remains imprisoned in the darkness. The Prophet (s.a.w.) said that after several sins are committed, the black dot in the heart starts to be covered with rust. With the rusting of the heart, the light of Allah does not shine forth from it or cannot penetrate it. Some of the scary hadith of the Prophet (s.a.w.) is shadowed in the early verses of the Qur'an. In *surah* al-Baqarah, Allah speaks of the three categories of human beings:

ٱلَّذِينَ يُؤْمِنُونَ بِٱلْغَيْبِ وَيُقِيمُونَ ٱلصَّلَوٰةَ وَمِمَّا رَزَقْنَـٰهُمْ يُنفِقُونَ ۝ وَٱلَّذِينَ يُؤْمِنُونَ بِمَآ أُنزِلَ إِلَيْكَ وَمَآ أُنزِلَ مِن قَبْلِكَ وَبِٱلْءَاخِرَةِ هُمْ يُوقِنُونَ ۝ أُو۟لَـٰٓئِكَ عَلَىٰ هُدًى مِّن رَّبِّهِمْ ۖ وَأُو۟لَـٰٓئِكَ هُمُ ٱلْمُفْلِحُونَ ۝

Those who believe in the unseen, establish prayer, and spend out of what We have provided them. And who believed what has been revealed to you, [O' Muḥammad], and what has been revealed before you, and of the Hereafter they are certain [in faith].

Those are upon [right] guidance from their Lord,
and it is those who are the successful.

(al-Baqarah, 2:3-5)

The first category is the believers; those who receive faith and accept it, those who believe in *al-ghayb*, and those who believe in what they should do and put it into practice.

إِنَّ ٱلَّذِينَ كَفَرُوا۟ سَوَآءٌ عَلَيْهِمْ ءَأَنذَرْتَهُمْ أَمْ لَمْ تُنذِرْهُمْ لَا يُؤْمِنُونَ ﴿٦﴾ خَتَمَ ٱللَّهُ عَلَىٰ قُلُوبِهِمْ وَعَلَىٰ سَمْعِهِمْ وَعَلَىٰٓ أَبْصَٰرِهِمْ غِشَٰوَةٌ وَلَهُمْ عَذَابٌ عَظِيمٌ ﴿٧﴾

Indeed those who disbelieve—it is all the same for them whether you warn them or you do not warn them—they will not believe. Allah has set a seal upon their hearts and upon their hearing, and over their vision is a veil. And for them is a great punishment.

(al-Baqarah, 2:6-7)

The second category is the people who recognise the truth, and immediately make the intent to be distant from it, and contradict its spirit after a deliberate understanding of it.

وَمِنَ ٱلنَّاسِ مَن يَقُولُ ءَامَنَّا بِٱللَّهِ وَبِٱلْيَوْمِ ٱلْءَاخِرِ وَمَا هُم بِمُؤْمِنِينَ ۝ يُخَـٰدِعُونَ ٱللَّهَ وَٱلَّذِينَ ءَامَنُوا۟ وَمَا يَخْدَعُونَ إِلَّآ أَنفُسَهُمْ وَمَا يَشْعُرُونَ ۝ فِى قُلُوبِهِم مَّرَضٌ فَزَادَهُمُ ٱللَّهُ مَرَضًا ۖ وَلَهُمْ عَذَابٌ أَلِيمٌۢ بِمَا كَانُوا۟ يَكْذِبُونَ ۝

And of the people are some who say, "We believe in Allah and the Last Day," but they are not believers. They [think to] deceive Allah and those who believe, but they deceive not except themselves and perceive [it] not. In their hearts is disease, so Allah has increased their disease; and for them is a painful punishment because they [habitually] used to lie.

(al-Baqarah, 2:8-10)

And in between are the hypocrites, those who meander between truth and falsehood, *khatama Allāhu ʿalā qulūbihim*, "They're the ones whose heart becomes stamped, sealed by Allah." That word perplexed the *ʿulama*. *Khatama Allāhu ʿalā qulūbihim*, means that it becomes covered in their sins that even though they hear and understand the truth, may even want the truth because their heart,

124

… فَلَمَّا زَاغُوٓاْ أَزَاغَ ٱللَّهُ قُلُوبَهُمْ … ۝

… And when they deviated, Allah caused their hearts to deviate…

(aṣ-Ṣaf, 61:5)

When their hearts departed from Allah (s.w.t.), He made their hearts irreparable to come back to the truth. So their heart becomes stamped. The *'ulama'* always wondered, why Allah may be the barrier. May Allah protect us. Could you imagine that Allah is the one who is barring our hearts from receiving the guidance that He sent for us to enliven it? Allah says in *surah* al-Anfal:

يَـٰٓأَيُّهَا ٱلَّذِينَ ءَامَنُواْ ٱسْتَجِيبُواْ لِلَّهِ وَلِلرَّسُولِ إِذَا دَعَاكُمْ لِمَا يُحْيِيكُمْ ۖ وَٱعْلَمُوٓاْ أَنَّ ٱللَّهَ يَحُولُ بَيْنَ ٱلْمَرْءِ وَقَلْبِهِۦ وَأَنَّهُۥٓ إِلَيْهِ تُحْشَرُونَ ۝

O' you who have believed, respond to Allah and to the Messenger when he calls you to that which gives you life. And know that Allah intervenes between a man and his heart and that to Him you will be gathered.

(al-Anfal, 8:24)

125

"O' you who believe, respond quickly to the message and the call of Allah and the messenger." When you are invited, called forward, or given advice to that which Allah and His messenger have been sent with, be wary, and be careful, Allah may become the barrier between an individual and their heart. If the response is given to us, the command is given to us by Allah to come to the path of Allah, and our heart detects it, recognises it, and then in a moment of lapse we choose willingly, wantingly, and intentionally to diverge from it, Allah (s.w.t.) then causes our own deeds to bar us from Him.

How do we become pure? How do we deoxidise? How do we remove the rust? How do we polish a heart if we are not willing to have the friction that is going to cause it to become better in the future? How can we have a heart that becomes cleansed if we are not willing to have the "why you brush, scrub you clean?" How can we have a heart that will be resilient if we don't want anything difficult in our life? If we do not want to sacrifice what we find dear? How can our heart grow and increase in its capacity to love and be loved, if we do not want to lose and at times be lost?

Allah sends us Nabi Muḥammad (s.a.w.), as a model and an example of purity. An example of the one who gained, but suffered and lost. The one who was uplifted, and then was humbled, in meaningful ways and in ways that at times seemed silly, but are important because they give us a complex understanding of our very nature in life. One of the times when the *sahabah* were so upset was when the camel owned by the Prophet (s.a.w.), had lost a race. At the times when they used to love racing and competition, Muḥammad's (s.a.w.) camel always came first. One day, his camel lost, and came second, so Muḥammad had to give his camel to a rider, and he would raise it in the desert with another rider. The *sahabah* were upset that his camel lost, since it is the Prophet (s.a.w.) as whatever he (s.a.w.) owns has to have the ascendancy. How could anything bad, and any misfortune happen, the *sahabah* thought. And the Prophet simply says one life-changing sentence for us, if we understand it, "It is right upon Allah that nothing is raised in this world except He lowers it."

> "The Messenger of Allah had a she-camel called Al-'Adba' which could not be beaten. One day a Bedouin came on a riding-camel and beat her (in a race). The Muslims were upset by that, and when he (s.a.w.) saw the expressions on their faces they said: 'O' Messenger of Allah, Al-'Adba' has been beaten.' He said: 'It is a right upon Allah that nothing is raised in this world except He lowers it.'"

(Sunan an-Nasa'i 3588)

Nothing becomes an icon. Nothing becomes at its peak, except eventually it will be humbled and brought down. *SubḥanAllāh*. Nobody ever climbs Everest and stays there. Imagine yourself arriving up there, and saying "I'm at the top of the world. I'm not leaving." That is at our own peril. What goes up must come down. *Allāhu akbar*. Allah says that He is the one who brought us into this world:

$$وَٱللَّهُ أَخْرَجَكُم مِّنْ بُطُونِ أُمَّهَـٰتِكُمْ لَا تَعْلَمُونَ شَيْئًا وَجَعَلَ لَكُمُ ٱلسَّمْعَ وَٱلْأَبْصَـٰرَ وَٱلْأَفْـِٔدَةَ ۙ لَعَلَّكُمْ تَشْكُرُونَ ﴿٧٨﴾$$

And Allah has extracted you from the wombs of your mothers not knowing a thing, and He made for you hearing and vision and hearts [i.e., intellect] that perhaps you would be grateful.

(an-Naḥl, 16:78)

We knew nothing when we were delivered into this world—we were wrapped into a shroud, into a beautiful display for our parents to hold, feed and teach us how to read, write, walk, move and act. And then we grow strong, and find our vigour; then we begin our transition towards our *akhirah*. May Allah seal all of our faith in Him. And as we endure that process of the up of life, the peak of life, remember the return, *Innā lillāhi wa innā ilayhi rāji'un.*

$$\ldots \quad إِنَّا لِلَّهِ وَإِنَّا إِلَيْهِ رَٰجِعُونَ ﴿١٥٦﴾$$

...*"Indeed we belong to Allah, and indeed to Him we will return."*

(al-Baqarah, 2:156)

Purity is in that recognition. What is going to purify our life is that there is this serene, peaceful, content, *riḍa* in the fact that there is no power, no might, no ability, and no strength, except that which is provided by Allah.

"The Messenger of Allah (s.a.w.) said to me: 'Be frequent in saying: "There is no might or power except by Allah, (*Lā ḥawla wa lā quwwata illā billāh*)." For verily, it is a treasure from the treasures of Paradise.'"

(Jami' at-Tirmidhi 3601)

It is an understanding that the totality of judgement is with Allah. I was leading my students in prayer, and *subhanAllāh,* I forgot how many *rak'ah.* I knew it was *ṣalah Zuhr.* As I finished the *ṣalah,* I knew I had messed up. I probably had only performed three *rak'ah, Allāhu akbar*. After the *ṣalah*, the students, especially the seniors behind me said, "Shaykh we were praying *Zuhr*." I said, "Me too." I was too shy. Did I make a big or a small mistake? Is it something we can correct with two *sujud* or do we need to start the *ṣalah* all over again? I looked at one of the boys who leads the *tarawiḥ* with me, who I taught the *fiqh* of *ṣalah*.

So I turned to him and said, "Muhammad, what do we do?" He answered, "Shaykh, you have to do it again." I said "OK." At that moment all the boys, especially the young ones, went "Ahh!" I was like, "O' Allah." How many years have I been leading these kids? *Masha'Allāh*. I made one mistake one time, which just cost them an extra ten minutes off their lunch. "Aww man, Shaykh taught us about *ṣalah*. He tells us all the time to concentrate, concentrate, now look at him." And at that moment, I remembered the *du'a'* of the Prophet (s.a.w.) that we make in the morning.

أَصْبَحْنَا وَأَصْبَحَ الْمُلْكُ لِلَّهِ وَالْحَمْدُ لِلَّهِ، لاَ إِلَهَ إِلاَّ اللَّهُ وَحْدَهُ لاَ شَرِيكَ لَهُ، لَهُ الْمُلْكُ وَلَهُ الْحَمْدُ وَهُوَ عَلَى كُلِّ شَيْءٍ قَدِيرٌ، رَبِّ أَسْأَلُكَ خَيْرَ مَا فِي هَذَا الْيَوْمِ وَخَيْرَ مَا بَعْدَهُ، وَأَعُوذُ بِكَ مِنْ شَرِّ مَا

فِي هَذَا الْيَوْمِ وَشَرِّ مَا بَعْدَهُ، رَبِّ أَعُوذُ بِكَ مِنَ الْكَسَلِ وَسُوءِ الْكِبَرِ، رَبِّ أَعُوذُ بِكَ مِنْ عَذَابٍ فِي النَّارِ وَعَذَابٍ فِي القَبْرِ.

Aṣbaḥnā wa aṣbaḥal-mulku lillāh, walḥamdu lillāh, lā ilāha illallāhu waḥdahu lā sharīka lah, lahul-mulku wa lahul-ḥamd, wa huwa ʿalā kulli shayʾin Qadīr. Rabbi asʾaluka khayra mā fī hādhal-yawmi wa khayra mā baʿdahu wa aʿūdhu bika min sharri mā fī hāthal-yawmi wa sharri mā baʿdahu, Rabbi aʿūdhu bika minal-kasali, wa sūʾil-kibar, Rabbi aʿūdhu bika min ʿadhābin fin-nāri wa ʿadhābin fil-qabr.

We have entered a new day and with it all dominion is Allah's. Praise is to Allah. None has the right to be worshipped but Allah alone, Who has no partner. To Allah belongs the dominion, and to Him is the praise and He is Able to do all things. My Lord, I ask You for the goodness of this day and of the days that come after it, and I seek refuge in You from the evil of this day and of the days that come after it. My Lord, I seek refuge in You from laziness and helpless old age. My Lord, I seek refuge in You

from the punishment of Hell-fire, and from the punishment of the grave.

(Hisn al-Muslim 77)

We woke up to find that all of the kingdoms belongs to Allah and *Alḥamdulillāh* for that. Could you imagine if we were accountable to others? Could you imagine if it wasn't Allah who judged you? My students did not even have the patience for ten minutes. Could you imagine if it was your father who judged you? Your mother, or even your wife? How beautiful it is that Allah is *al-Mālik*. That it is Allah who is the judge. The one who is *ar-Raḥmān*, who is *ar-Raḥīm*, *al-Ghaffūr*, *ar-Raūf*, the gentle, the forgiving, the pardoning. With Allah, we sleep when we should be awake. We take when we should give. We hurt when we should heal. Allah says:

> "…O' My servants, you sin by night and by day,
> and I forgive all sins, so seek forgiveness of Me and
> I shall forgive you…"

(Ṣaḥih Muslim 2577a)

We are sinful in our day and in our night. And if we were to come to Him (s.w.t.) and ask for His forgiveness, He will forgive us.

132

Jannah was not made for the whole, for the unblemished. *Jannah* was never destined for Adam (a.s.) before sin. *Jannah* was not fit for Adam (a.s.) if he did not struggle to become better, to earn it. *Jannah* is for us, who seek a better purity to more than we are today. Our life is about purifying, bettering, increasing, assisting, healing, trying, just trying, not even succeeding. Allah does not value you on what you accomplished. He values you on the intention and the attempt. *Ar-Raḥmān, Ar-Raḥīm*. So it becomes our duty to think of how to be better. When we critique the sunnah, we begin to develop a psychology of redemption that is built on three simple cornerstones.

Self-Critique

First is self-awareness, self critique, *muḥasabah*. Taking stops of your day and night, of your week, of your month, looking at your success and wondering, "How can I flourish and increase them?" Looking at your failings and wondering, "What pathways can I take, and who can assist me in eliminating them?" Being real with yourself. Sitting at the edge of your bed before you set yourself to sleep, and finding fault with one or two of your indiscretions. And just admitting your mistake between you and Allah, admitting that you are flawed and careless, and you are mistaken in your approach. Then ask with genuineness to have the strength to do better.

اللَّهُمَّ أَعِنِّيْ عَلَى ذِكْرِكَ وَشُكْرِكَ وَحُسْنِ عِبَادَتِكَ

O' Allah help me in remembering You, in thanking You, and to worship You in the most excellent manner.

(Hiṣn al-Muslim 59)

O' Allah help me to remember you. O' Allah help me so that when I am standing at something that I want but I should not have, help me to remember you. Help me so that I can bring you to mind, to heart. Help me to thank you more for what I have that I overlooked, so that I can turn my gaze away from what others have been blessed with, so that I won't crave anything and devalue what exists with me. That if I understood it, I would never take it for granted.

Muʿadh (bin Jabal) (r.a.) reported:

Messenger of Allah (s.a.w.) held my hand and said, "O' Muʿadh, By Allah, I love you and advise you not to miss supplicating after every *ṣalah* (prayer) saying: *'Allāhumma aʿinni aʿlā dhikrika wa shukrika, wa husni ʿibādatika,*' (O' Allah, help me remember You, expressing gratitude to You and worship You in the best manner)".

(Riyaḍ as-Saliḥin 384)

Wa ḥusni ʿibādatika. And then I can become better—better in my *ʿibadah,* better in my love, in fear and hope, better in the performance of the physical worship of you. Better in the internal process of cleansing of my heart, and of my being. The Prophet (s.a.w.) sat with the *saḥabah* in his *masjid.* And he said, "The next man through that door is from the people of *Jannah.*" Everybody seated there regretted that they were with him. And everybody seated there hoped that it would be their brother or their friend, their wife or somebody they love. Everybody had a thought of 'if it cannot be me, then I hope it's them', then some unfamiliar yet normal person entered.

'Abdullah ibn 'Umar, the elite of the *saḥabah.* He was one of the major reporters of the hadith of Rasulullah (s.a.w.), the son of 'Umar ibn al-Khaṭṭab. He was the one who critiqued, followed and learned the sunnah of the Prophet (s.a.w.) step after step. He followed the unknown man to know what made that man worthy of the truthful promise of the Prophet. He spied on the man for a whole day, but saw nothing important. He went to work, then went back home.

Nothing. No Qur'an, nothing. Perhaps this man's strength is his nights. So he complained to the man, said that he had a problem with his father and asked if he could seek shelter at the man's house? It is the right upon Muslim to seek shelter. The man said, "yes". The man offered him a nice meal, and he retired into his bed to sleep. 'Abdullah ibn'Umar said that the man never stood up for long hours for prayer. He sat there wondering when the man would wake up. While everyone was busy doing the *tahajjud*, this man was sleeping. What happened? When the *Fajr* came, they prayed, and the man started his day again. 'Abdullah could not control himself anymore, so he told the man, "Listen, the Prophet (s.a.w.) said that the next man to enter the door is from the people of *Jannah*, and you happened to be that man. What do you do that makes you worthy of this?" He said, "I don't count myself as significant, only that every night as I am about to sleep, *'Akhraj min qalbik'*, I force out of my heart, any *shahna'* (lustful), anger, jealousy or hate that I have to another. And I put it with Allah. I say 'Allah, I let you handle it for me, I don't sit here angry, obsessed and conniving, thinking night after night, I push it out of my heart.'"

It is that purity of the heart that made you worthy of that place in *Jannah*.

Anas ibn Malik (r.a.) reported:

He was sitting with the Messenger of Allah (s.a.w.) and he said, "Coming upon you now is a man from the people of Paradise." So a man came from the helpers whose beard looked disarrayed by the water from ablution, and he was carrying both of his shoes with his left hand. The next day the Prophet repeated the same words, and the helpers came in the same condition. The third day the Prophet repeated the same again, and the man from the helpers showed up in the same condition. When the Messenger of Allah stood up to leave, 'Abdullah ibn 'Umar ibn Al-As followed the man and asked him, "I have quarrelled with my father and I have sworn not to enter my home for three days. May I stay with you?" He said, "Yes."

'Abdullah ibn 'Umar ibn Al-As stayed three nights with him but never saw him praying at night, and whenever he went to bed, he would remember Allah and rest until he woke up for morning prayer. Abdullah said that he never heard anything but good from his mouth. When three nights had passed and he did not see anything special about his actions, 'Abdullah ibn 'Umar asked him, "O' servant of Allah, I have not quarrelled with my father nor have I cut relations with him. I heard the Messenger of Allah say three times that a man from the people of Paradise was coming to us, and then you came. So I thought I should stay with you and see what you are doing that I should follow, but I did not see you do anything special. What is the reason that the Messenger of Allah spoke highly of you?" The man said, "It is as you have seen." When 'Abdullah was about to leave, the man said, "It is as you have seen, except that I do not find fraud in my soul towards the Muslims, and I do not envy anyone because of the good that Allah has given them."

(Musnad Aḥmad, 12286)

Allah mentions in the Qur'an:

$$\text{وَنَزَعْنَا مَا فِى صُدُورِهِم مِّنْ غِلٍّ تَجْرِى مِن تَحْتِهِمُ الْأَنْهَـٰرُ ... ﴿٤٣﴾}$$

"And We will have removed whatever is within their breasts of resentment, [while] flowing beneath them are rivers..."

(al-Aʿraf, 7:43)

For us to enter *Jannah*, one of the primary purposes

of the Hellfire for a believer to endure it, is that Allah purges, He removes anger, rancour and jealousy from our hearts towards others, so they enter into paradise, *Ikhwana* (brethren amongst each other).

For you to enter *Jannah*, try to just sit and monitor your heart, sit and say to yourself, " This is a problem that I have, and I need to work on it. This is where I need to improve." Psychologists and therapists will tell you the same thing. They will tell you, "Listen, you need to have self-reflection, and you need to understand what your issues are, and not just what the issues of others in response or towards you, or what triggers you. You need to sit with yourself and just focus on "Me, myself and my place in the world." Ask, "What can I do to become better?"

'Umar (r.a.) used to say that Allah bless those who know their capabilities. Allah's mercy follows a person who knows their limitations, who knows their success, their strengths, knows their failings and their failure and begins to take judgement in accordance with them. And 'Umar (r.a.) would say on the *mimbar* on Jumu'ah prayer, when he was the *Amir al-Mu'minin*:

…"Reckon with yourselves before you are reckoned
with, and prepare for the Greatest Inquisition. The

reckoning of the Day of Judgement is only light for the one who reckoned with himself in the world."…

(Jami' at-Tirmidhi, 2459)

Nothing is hidden before Allah. Self-critique is meant to identify what it is that we need to improve, what it is that we need to step back from, and what it is that we need to increase in doing good in, in order to add vigour and have greater health to the vibrancy of our spiritual heart.

Self-Control

Self-control is a lost sunnah of the Prophet Muḥammad (s.a.w.). Self-control was something that the Prophet (s.a.w.) tried to teach us in almost every aspect of our worship to Allah (s.w.t.) for instance in the *tahajjud* prayer. It takes great self-control to wake up for *tahajjud* at night, even when we are travelling. 'A'ishah (r.a.) said in a hadith:

Do not give up prayer at night, for the Messenger of Allah (s.a.w.) would not leave it. Whenever he fell ill or lethargic, he would offer it sitting.

(Sunan Abi Dawud 1307)

She tells us that the *tahajjud* prayer was something that

the Prophet (s.a.w.) never left. Whether he (s.a.w.) was at home or was travelling, whether he was in good health or ill, he (s.a.w.) always did his *tahajjud* prayer. Thus, self-control is a direct correlation between our *'ibadah* to Allah (s.w.t.) in our private setting, in our independency, and in our non-recognition—where people do not know as a measure of our own ability to control ourselves and to regiment our life in that which will also be in our public spheres.

How to develop self-control? By beginning to worship Allah (s.w.t.) better. By taking count of how many sunnah *mu'akkadah* (prayer which was continuously performed and almost never abandoned by the Prophet) we do every day. Some *sunnah mu'akkadah* prayer that we can do every day is:

1. 2 *rak'ah* before *Fajr*.

2. 4 *rak'ah* before *Zuhr*.

3. 2 *rak'ah* after *Zuhr*.

4. 2 *rak'ah* after *Maghrib*.

5. 2 *rak'ah* after *'Isha'*

Salatul witr was also a prayer that the Prophet (s.a.w.) never missed even in war. In Mazhab Hanafi, the *witr* prayer is *wajib*.

Self-control is a learned behaviour.

Self-control is a learned behaviour.

Pay heed to this advice; that self-control is a learned behaviour. I would like to give an example pertaining to children however this is not about children who are on the spectrum. In general, some children have been socialised without self-control. For example, there was a four-year-old kid at the mall who wanted a toy but his mother did not let him and asked him to put it back in an angry tone. The child's response was that he was not going to put it back. The mother tried to take the toy but the kid ran, and so she ran after him as well. When she took away the toy, the child was wailing and throwing a tantrum on the floor. The mother gave him something to eat to soothe him, but the kid threw the food away. Fast forward to thirty years later; the boy is now a man and is married and at a moment of conflict he said *ṭalaq, ṭalaq, ṭalaq* like a machine gun.

A brother I knew told me that he said *ṭalaq* (divorce) to his wife a number of times, like a machine gun. He said it was because he had gotten angry and that is why he said *ṭalaq*. I said "Who says it when they are happy?" He said he had lost his mind. So I asked him, "could you drive that day to work? He said, "Yes." I asked, "did you go to work that day?" He said, "Yes." In fact, he mentioned that everything went smoothly for him that day—his work, his meeting. Only for those twelve minutes when he said *talaq* was the only moment where he had lost his mind. I asked him if he remembered how many times he said *talaq* but he could not recall as he lost count, because he said it too many times. That is why, the secular government of India actually passed a law against the Mazhab Hanafi, pertaining to divorce. This is because in Mazhab Hanafi, saying *talaq* three times in a row or saying it ten times, is the same— meaning that the marriage is already broken then and there. Three *talaq* in one setting, in one moment, is counted as three individual *talaq* and so you are not a husband and wife anymore. This is causing havoc in India because most of the brothers say *talaq* like a machine gun. That is why the Indian government stepped in as they found other opinions in Islam as well. They had to stop the law of divorce because it was destroying society.

Furthermore, those of us who work in schools, especially with younger children, are put in a situation where we have to deal with children who respond to authority the way their parents have indoctrinated them. Therefore, children who only understand yelling as a form of seriousness, disregard anything a person says in a normal conversation. This is because they have been taught and socialised in a way that yelling is a form of seriousness. Hence, unless the other party (the one who talks in a normal manner) gets angry with them to explain their mistake, they will only be taking more time to do whatever they want.

That is why self-control is a learned and taught behaviour. Self-discipline and self-regulation are one of the aims of each one of our fundamental pillars of Islam. If we were to look at *ṣalah*—the self-control is to wake ourselves up, to make *wuḍu'* and then to stand up in prayer. Thus, learned behaviour moulds self-control. Another example of having self-control by learning is for instance learning that if the water is not enough for survival, *tayammum* can be done in order to still carry out the *ʿibadah* of prayer. There is always a process. There is always a way to work through the problems just as we are taught by the Prophet (s.a.w.)—like to make *tayammum* if there is no water. If our arm is cut or injured, then we have to just put a bandage on it and precede with *wuḍu'* as the bandage will already avoid from the injury from feeling stung. Self-control—learned behaviour was always meant to simplify the problems that we face through knowledge and to never abandon it. In addition, *ṣalah* was also meant to teach people to leave their selling and commerce behind to answer the call of prayer, to go for *jamaʿah*. Furthermore, it was never conceivable that a man would not pray *Fajr* and *Isha'* except in the masjid.

A man, according to the majority opinion, says that

it is *wajib* for a man to pray *Fajr* and *'Isha'* in the mosque. However, men nowadays say it is hard as times are tough. I want to explain an example that the Prophet (s.a.w.) gave us, about the story of Bani Sa'd. They were from the people of Quba and they lived there. When the Prophet (s.a.w.) moved and established the *masjid*, the people would walk for every *Fajr* in the dark, for an hour and thirty minutes to pray *jama'ah* with the Prophet (s.a.w.). Afterwards, they would walk back to their fields to do their work. For *Zuhr*, in the heat of the sun, they would walk to the *masjid* for prayer and stay there until *'Asr* as it was too hot to go back. After *'Asr*, they would go back home and then come back for Maghrib and *'Isha'*. Every day, they took three trips and they became tired of it. So the people had a family/tribal meeting to discuss the matter. They wanted to solve the problem however they were not wealthy enough to buy horses that would save them time to go to the *masjid*. So the only solution they could think of was to pack up their stuff and live in the *masjid* of the Prophet (s.a.w.). That was the only logical solution they could come up with. They were not going to let the tiredness make them pray at their homes. That was the way they understood life.

Allah revealed in *surah* Yasin, that He (s.w.t.) even writes down our *waathārahu*, footprints. Allah writes down and counts the footsteps that we have taken when we are doing good deeds when we are obeying Allah's command and He (s.w.t.) will open for us happiness for it. Thus, when the people of Bani Sa'd went back to their orchards, they were able to make an abundance of profit with the fruits they planted, as Allah blessed them for it. Their tribe became wealthy and everyone owned a horse. They all rode their horses to the *masjid* of the Prophet (s.a.w.). And so, sacrifice and the ability to persevere for the sake of Allah will give us blessings and great profit in return. Therefore, we need to control ourselves. We need to control our *salah*, *siyam* (fasting), thirst, hunger, eyes, ears, conversations, evenings and nights, *sabr* (patience), and more. All these deeds are a part of developing self-control. The main aim of it is to develop growth, strength and dominance over ourselves.

Self-Sacrifice

As we ascend from looking into our hearts, our behaviour, taking account of ourselves, and planning bigger achievements for the future—as well as setting out a plan of self-control, self-moderation, and self-regulation, we then come to the third step of self-sacrifice. If we are a taker and not a giver, an insulter, and are not willing to amend and augment our demeanour—then what are we willing to give unto others to make up for the wrong deeds we did to them and ourselves?

Self-sacrifice becomes one of the final steps in a psychology of purity. And in any relationship, not only with Allah (s.w.t.), whenever we have done something to incur the wrath of another, or wronged another person; taken the *ḥaq* (rights) of another, and insulted another, we must take the following three steps:

1. Assessing ourselves in terms of where we were wrong and right.

2. What are we going to do to protect ourselves from doing it again?

3. What are the tools that we need to develop in order to not make the same wrong decision, or fall back into the wrong things and to make up for those who have grieved due to our mistakes?

This can be in terms of a husband to his wife or even son/daughter to their parents. Let me give you an example. A brother I knew in Melbourne told me that could not take his wife anymore. I asked him why as he *Masha'Allāh*, has a beautiful family and children. He said it was because his wife kept putting him down. His wife kept mentioning that everyone she knows has a house they own but he did not give her one as promised. And so, the wife keeps mentioning property values due to it too. I asked the brother, "Did you promise her that you would give her a house?" He said

"Yes." I told him then that the wife was right.

I asked him again, "Did you promise her?" He said, "Yes."

"Does she deserve it?" He said, "Yes."

"Are you able to afford it?" He said, "Yes."

"Then why have you not given her a house and fulfilled your words?" He said, "I don't know."

I asked him, "Is it because you just want to show her that you are the boss? That you are a macho man?"

And then he says "But she shouldn't humiliate me Shaykh."

I mentioned in the earlier part of the book in regards to humiliation, *dhanab*. The question is who humiliates who initially? The answer is ourselves. When we do wrong, we invite humiliation towards ourselves. How the wife was with her husband, the brother was not right as well. If I were to sit with her and talk, I would condemn her behaviour. However, when I am with the brother, I must condemn his behaviour as well because he is in the wrong too. The brother used the word hate to condemn his wife as well. Hence, I would like to highlight this part. The Prophet (s.a.w.) mentioned in a hadith that if a man sees in a woman something he hates, he should then acknowledge something he loves about her:

A believing man should not hate a believing woman; if he dislikes one of her characteristics, he will be pleased with another.

(Ṣaḥīḥ Muslim 1468b)

I have to tell the brother that what he said was wrong as well. That it is a corruption for his soul. That it is an error in his ways. He has to self-regulate, self-critique, self-assess and now self-sacrifice. Therefore, sometimes we need to look from another perspective, from another person's lenses and vantage point. And that is entirely the sunnah of our Nabi Muḥammad (s.a.w.).

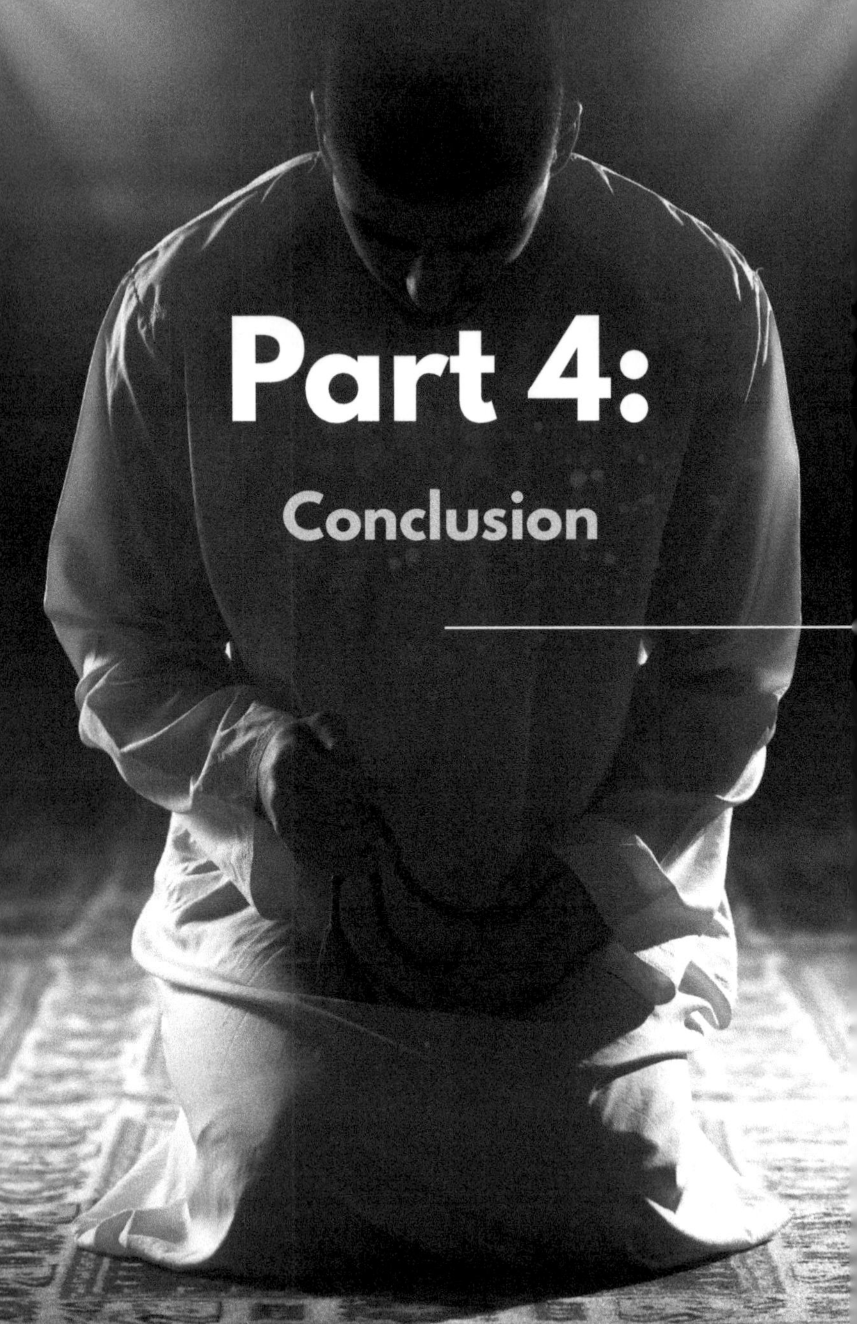
Part 4:
Conclusion

Chapter 12:
Your Lord is
ar-Raḥman

One of the most beautiful names of Allah is *ar-Rahman*. It is also one of the most misunderstood names of Allah. Most people, when they are in trouble, they say *Ya Rahman*. Their assumption is that Allah being merciful means that Allah will also be gentle and non-injurious to them. In fact, the definition of the name *Rahman* includes the one who causes harm for the overall good. The one who can cause you pain because it is what's better for you. For example, a mother has *rahmah* for her child. If he comes near a stove, she might have to censor him. She might have to hold him back. She has to settle him down. "Hey, don't go there again." Sometimes you have to be tough out of your love for him. A doctor may show *rahmah* by cutting off a limb that we value but if it is not removed, it will cause greater harm to the other parts of the body. Allah (s.w.t.) can take from us our *rizq*. Allah may take from us a moment of joy or happiness or a blessing that was gifted as an act of *rahmah*.

Therefore, in the story of Musa (a.s.) and al-Khidr (a.s.) in regard to the killing of a young boy; al-Khidr says to Musa (a.s.), "I was ordered by Allah to take this young man's life." It is a mercy from Allah (s.w.t.). The parents of that young man will never know that the loss of their child was for their benefit. One of the mysteries of this *surah* is that Musa (a.s.) does not go to the parents and say "Hey, listen, I'm Musa (a.s.). This is a good guy, al-Khidr. We heard that your child is missing…" because the parents will mourn that child.

The parents will be upset for the rest of their life for the loss of a child that they brought into the world, even though he was difficult. Even though he was a burden; even though in the knowledge of Allah (s.w.t.), he was going to push them away from Islam, but Allah valued their *iman*. There are things that Allah (s.w.t.) in his *raḥmah* challenges us with.

وَلَقَدْ قَالَ لَهُمْ هَـٰرُونُ مِن قَبْلُ يَـٰقَوْمِ إِنَّمَا فُتِنتُم بِهِۦ ۖ وَإِنَّ رَبَّكُمُ ٱلرَّحْمَـٰنُ فَٱتَّبِعُونِى وَأَطِيعُوٓا۟ أَمْرِى ﴿٩٠﴾

And Aaron had already told them before [the return of Moses], "O' my people, you are only being tested by it, and indeed, your Lord is the Most Merciful, so follow me and obey my order."

(Ṭaha, 20:90)

And as we invoke Allah's mercy into our lives, do not ever assume that it means relief in the way we desire it. We are not in control. We thank Allah (s.w.t.) that the *Mulk* (Kingdom) is with Him. *Alḥamdulillāh*, in the *qadr* of Allah and *qaḍa'* of Allah for us as believers. *Alḥamdulillāh*, that Allah is the One who is in charge of our life.

Chapter 13: The Straight Path

The *sirat* is:

- Straight

- Wide

- Clear

- Direct

- Exclusive

- Guaranteed

1. It is straight.

As you and I walk the *Siratal-Mustaqim*, that opening verse of the Qur'an, I want you to meditate on the meaning of that word. *Ihdinas-Sirat*. Lead us to the straight path. The word *sirat*—its initial meaning is straight; there is no meandering. From point A to point B, it incurs the least cost and the shortest, least injurious path. Even though we might see that there is a shortcut, if we cut right and then come back, we might think it is better—it is not. A *sirat* is free of curbs and detours. It is meant to cut through expediently through the known methodology of the prophets of the past and it is finalised with our Nabi Muhammad (s.a.w.).

2. It is wide.

In the Arabic language, the word *ṣiraṭ* means *wasiah*. It got room. No one's gonna push you out. Nobody has room to put despair in your heart. Nobody has the right to put you in a place where you feel "I cannot belong", even as a sinner on my path to *Jannah*. The *ṣiraṭ* is accommodating and welcoming. Anyone who seeks to call to the *ṣiraṭ* by narrowing it—in a way that was not narrowed by Allah (s.w.t.) or by pushing those who were welcomed by the Prophet (s.a.w.) off it—then they are the ones who become obstacles upon it.

3. It is clear of impediments and obstructions.

As *ṣiraṭ* the word that you ask in *Surah* al-Fatiḥah is that it is clear of impediments and obstructions. The Prophet (s.a.w.) said:

Abu Darda' said:

"The Messenger of Allah (s.a.w.) came out to us when we were speaking of poverty and how we feared it. He said: 'Is it poverty that you fear? By the One in Whose Hand is my soul, (the delights and luxuries of) this world will come to you in plenty, and nothing will cause the heart of anyone of you to deviate except that. By Allah, I am leaving you upon something like *Bayda* (white, bright, clear path) the night and day of which are the same.'"

(Sunan ibn Majah 5)

Whether it is night or day, it is bright. We do not need to worry—if we stick to the Qur'an, if we hold onto the sunnah, if we follow the *'ulama'*. We do not need to worry—if we do not make our *hawa'*, our desire our guide in life; if we navigate with the map book sent to us by Allah Almighty.

$$\text{أَلَا يَعْلَمُ مَنْ خَلَقَ وَهُوَ ٱللَّطِيفُ ٱلْخَبِيرُ}$$

Does He who created not know, while He is the Subtle, the Aware?

(al-Mulk, 67:14)

Is not The Creator The Best Suited to give His creation their manual of learning and trust? It is a clear, unequivocal and self-evident path to those who search for it, not just with their eyes but with the truth that they seek with their heart.

4. It is the most direct.

The concept of the word *sirat* in *lughah*? In the linguistic sense, it is that it is direct. Direct to where? Direct from the *dunya* to the *Jannah*. The Prophet (s.a.w.)—he would say these amazing things. He would say, "If a person was to read *Ayatul Kursi* after every *ṣalah*, they are in *Jannah* already. They just have not died yet. *SubḥanAllāh*. You performed *Zuhr*, you read *Ayatul Kursi*, *Aṣr*—*Ayatul Kursi*, *Maghrib*—*Ayatul Kursi*. Your place in *Jannah* is sure but you are still here, in *dunya*. It is a direct path to a better place with Allah (s.w.t.).

5. It is exclusive.

وَأَنَّ هَـٰذَا صِرَٰطِى مُسْتَقِيمًا فَٱتَّبِعُوهُ ۖ وَلَا تَتَّبِعُوا۟ ٱلسُّبُلَ فَتَفَرَّقَ بِكُمْ عَن سَبِيلِهِۦ ۚ ذَٰلِكُمْ وَصَّىٰكُم بِهِۦ لَعَلَّكُمْ تَتَّقُونَ ﴿١٥٣﴾

And, [moreover], this is My path, which is straight, so follow it; and do not follow [other] ways, for you will be separated from His way. This has He instructed you that you may become righteous.

(al-An'am, 6:153)

The word *ṣirat* is exclusive. This *ṣirat* of Mine is upright, it is straight, it is the clear path, it is wide, it is direct, it is encompassing. Don't follow any other road. It is exclusive. It is the only way. There is no detour. There is no other path or passage that will make us arrive at *Jannah*. We do not believe in the universality of faith. We do not believe that there is equal measure. "As long as I'm a good person, that's all that matters." No. There is a *Siraṭal-Mustaqim*.

صِرَٰطَ ٱلَّذِينَ أَنْعَمْتَ عَلَيْهِمْ

The path of those upon whom You have bestowed favor,

The path of those who came before me, whose footsteps I put my foot in

غَيْرِ ٱلْمَغْضُوبِ عَلَيْهِمْ

not of those who have earned [Your] anger

Not the path of those who earned your anger. Not the path of those who learned the truth and choose not to follow it.

وَلَا ٱلضَّآلِّيـنَ

or of those who are astray.

Not the path who knows that there is truth, but does not search for it, and wants to remain in their ignorance, unwilling to bend to truth, unwilling to adopt faith and its reality.

(al-Fatiḥah, 1:7)

6. It is guaranteed.

Finally, the *sirat* is guaranteed. The Prophet (s.a.w.) used to make *du'a'* in the night.

اللَّهُمَّ لَكَ الْحَمْدُ، أَنْتَ نُورُ السَّمَاوَاتِ وَالأَرْضِ وَمَنْ فِيهِنَّ، وَلَكَ الْحَمْدُ، أَنْتَ قَيَّامُ السَّمَاوَاتِ وَالأَرْضِ، وَلَكَ الْحَمْدُ أَنْتَ رَبُّ السَّمَاوَاتِ وَالأَرْضِ وَمَنْ فِيهِنَّ، أَنْتَ الْحَقُّ، وَوَعْدُكَ الْحَقُّ، وَلِقَاؤُكَ الْحَقُّ، وَالْجَنَّةُ حَقٌّ، وَالنَّارُ حَقٌّ، وَالسَّاعَةُ حَقٌّ. اللَّهُمَّ لَكَ أَسْلَمْتُ، وَبِكَ آمَنْتُ، وَعَلَيْكَ تَوَكَّلْتُ، وَإِلَيْكَ أَنَبْتُ، وَبِكَ خَاصَمْتُ، وَإِلَيْكَ حَاكَمْتُ، فَاغْفِرْ لِي مَا قَدَّمْتُ وَمَا أَخَّرْتُ، وَمَا أَسْرَرْتُ وَمَا أَعْلَنْتُ، أَنْتَ إِلَهِي، لَا إِلَهَ إِلَّا أَنْتَ.

O' Allah, Yours is the praise. You are the light of the heavens and the earth and whoever is in them. Yours is the praise. You are the Lord of the heavens and the earth and whoever is in them. You are the Truth and Your promise is true and the meeting with You is true. The Garden is true and the Fire is true and the Hour is true. O Allah, I have surrendered to You and I have believed in You. I have trusted in You and I repent to You. I argue by You and I have come to You for judgement. Forgive me my past and future wrong actions, what I conceal and what I show. You are My God. There is no god but You.

(Al-Adab Al-Mufrad 697)

May Allah (s.w.t.) allow us to hold firm to the *Siratal-Mustaqim*. May Allah (s.w.t.) make us from those who are upon its wide, direct, exclusive, straight path to *Jannah*. May Allah (s.w.t.) make us those who are willing to criticise ourselves, to hear the truth for what it is so that we adopt it and follow it, to hear falsehood for what it is, so that we can recognise it and be distant from it. May Allah (s.w.t.) brighten our days and our nights with the sunnah of the Prophet (s.a.w.). may Allah (s.w.t.) assist us against the cravings of our own soul when they go against the teaching of our Prophet (s.a.w.). May Allah (s.w.t.) help us against the whisperings of the *shaytan* and protect our homes from his evil unseen influence. May Allah (s.w.t.) protect us from the *shayatinil ins* (devils from humankind) who walk amongst us, who seek to lead us away from a path of righteousness and guidance. We ask Allah (s.w.t.) to bring our families and homes together, to allow those whose hearts are aggrieved with each other to find peace and resolve in the sunnah of the Prophet (s.a.w.). We ask Allah (s.w.t.) to make us all of those who are reformed, those who are healing from sin. And that when we fall folly and back into it, that you give us *tawbah* (repentance) before our return to you, O' Allah.

We ask You O' *Arhamar-rahimin*, to send Your *rahmah* upon those who have departed that we love in our life and in our days that we miss. We ask You O' *Arhamar-rahimin*, to bless those who remain with us, with the vigour and the intention of pleasing You O' Allah. We ask You Allah to send Your support and divine assistance upon each and every one of us who makes *du'a'* for You O' Allah. O' Allah, there are those of us who have *du'a'* that nobody knows but You O' Allah. Answer the *du'a'* of the *muhtajin* (the needy). We ask You O' Allah, answer the *du'a'* of the *masakin* (the poor).

O' Allah, we grovel and beg of You to grant us what none can grant but You, O' Allah. We ask You O' Allah, to give us prayer in the night and fasting in the day; reading and memorising of the Qur'an and with our families and generations to come. We ask You O' Allah, to make us protectors of the *deen* of the Prophet Muḥammad (s.a.w.), to honour us with his sunnah, in its word, in its intent and in our practice. We ask You O' Allah, to make us *imam* while we live and until our death, O' Allah. We ask You to give us the death of *shuhada' aṣ-ṣalihin*. We pray O' Allah, that You bless us with an accepted time that we have spent together, that it is a *raḥmah* and *ṣadaqah* that we have exchanged upon.

We pray that Allah (s.w.t.) blesses my home and your homes in ways that we did not know are missing. We pray that Allah (s.w.t.) grants us what we did not know we should ask of Him. And that Allah (s.w.t.) protects us from what we did not know we needed help and assistance against. We pray that Allah (s.w.t.) grants us the *shafa'ah* (intercession) of our Nabi Muḥammad (s.a.w.).

Questions &
Answers

QUESTION 1: My husband cheated on me multiple times. Currently, I'm struggling to figure out what is best for my family. And so, my question is how do we know if someone has sincerely repented and will never go back to his old habits?

A. I cannot give an answer to the specific question you have asked and the reason for that is because our *shariah* is very specific. Thus, something that is specific cannot be discussed in its generality. So, I will answer in a general manner instead. If someone was to come to me as a qualified mediator, as an *imam* who specialises in therapy with couples, I will say to them to not take the man or woman back—who has committed the sin multiple times knowingly, unless perhaps they have gone through a regimented clinical and spiritual process of redemption. There is no walking back into someone's life whom you have wronged with just a *"I'm sorry."* Being sorry does not help to fix the problem. And so, what is required is that there is intervention on a variety of levels.

Are there people who can reform themselves and be better? Yes.

Is it possible? Yes, absolutely.

Is it something that can be done in our modern times? Yes, but there are also going to be more frank discussions, and a greater level of trust that needs to be displayed.

The one who reforms and repents has to have greater transparencies, changes in lifestyle, and abandoning of old ways and old friends. There is a whole life paradigm shift if the person is invested in reforming and having a future with the family—they are willing to give up the pathway that is not the *ṣirat*. They should *want* to be on the *ṣirat*. Furthermore, it cannot just be done in a 'hush-hush manner' where we do not want our family to know as there has to be levels of transparency within a circle of trust—which probably includes a therapist, doctors, and perhaps sometimes a qualified *imam* as well. The process includes quite a number of people to help in so many aspects such as the addiction of the sin. That is just the general answer and not the specific answer to the question.

QUESTION 2: When we are faced with a certain difficulty, how do we know that we are being tested or punished?

A. Having difficulties is a natural process of life. 'Ali (r.a.) mentioned a very important statement regarding this. He mentioned that if the situation in our life, whether good or bad, brings us closer to Allah then it is *ibtilla'* (trials and tests); it is a test from Allah (s.w.t.) to strengthen and increase our faith. However, if the situation, whether good or bad, leads us away from Allah, leads us further into sin and makes us become more rebellious than before, then it is a punishment from Allah (s.w.t.). One of the ways Allah can punish us with is wealth and health that we waste in that which is immoral. Another way that Allah can punish us is by destroying the family we have built, where all our loved ones are taken away from our lives.

Sometimes, we assume that the test has to mean that we will be in darkness or in hardship. But we have to remember that all tests are put upon us to strengthen the *iman*. Allah tests us in our *iman* and increases it. At times, having good things makes it more difficult to pass the test rather than the test of losing something we value. When the things or person who is valuable are taken away, we become among the one who says to Allah,

"Allah please return it to me." "O'Allah assist and help me." However, after Allah opens the *Jannah* to all doers of the group, we become heedless.We build a family that then we destroy thereafter, and it is taken away from us. All of these are things sometimes we assume that the test has to be in darkness or in hardship.

Imam ibn Qayyim says that Allah tests us in our *iman* and with the tests we grow with our *iman*. with good things is more difficult of a test to pass than for Allah to take from us the things we value because when something is taken from you, you would plead Allah saying, "O' Allah, return it to me." "O' Allah, help me, O' Allah, assist me." But when Allah opens to you the doors of all good, you become *ghafil*—you become heedless. If Allah did not love me, why do I have this? Why am I driving this? Why am I working there? Why am I living? Why am I secure? Why am I healthy? If Allah does not favour me, why do I have all of this? So Allah (s.w.t.) tests in happiness and in sorrow, in open and in confinement. If anything, any situation in life brings you closer to Allah, it is an *ibtilla'* that is honouring to you by Allah, and purifying of your sins. If anything happens to you that leads you to rebellion against Allah, to distrust Allah, to be angry with Allah, to lack *riḍa* with Allah then it is a punishment from Allah (s.w.t.) and does not earn merits or rewards.

QUESTION 3: Thank you for sharing with us the three psychology of redemption—self-control, self-critique, and self-sacrifice. How do we not go overboard? Because when we have too much self-critique, we will become doubtful of ourselves. And if there is too much self-sacrifice, we might do something that is beyond what we can do. If there is too much self-control, we would then just want to be in control and will become anxious as well. So my question is, how do we balance it out?

A. That is a very good question. And it would be a very good question if it was for other than errors that we already identified. When we are speaking about self-critique, developing self-control, and then developing self-sacrifice, it is in something that we know we need to change. For example, the very first question that we were asked. Somebody who for example stepped out of the *halal* and did the *haram*. There must be self-accountability.

It is not just "What have I done that is hurting my wife?" or "What do people think?". It is now between that person and themselves. There needs to be self-accounting, self-realisation, self-awareness of the tragedy of their mistake. The self-control now needs to be "I need to get rid of this phone." "I need to get rid of this friend." "I need to not travel on my own." "I need to not be in this work environment that maybe I met this person in." "I need to control the things that relate to that matter." Then the third is: "What am I going to do to make it up to those I have wronged? How am I going to prove not just with tokenism? What am I going to sacrifice to let my family, my children and community?" Know that this is a change, that now there are KPIs or key performance indexes. "OK, I have met this, I am transitioning to this." It is not just, "Let's go to *'umrah*, kiss and make up."

So *jazakallāhu khayr.* I appreciate your question in highlighting that this needs to be in a confine of a particular situation and issue that is identified. It is not just I sit there and be like, "I hate everything about my life. I hate everything that I'm doing wrong." There is a place for self-critique, but there is a place for having hope and love for ourselves between us and Allah (s.w.t.). Thanks for highlighting the important distinction.

QUESTION 4: You said something about, "When we sin, we need to do something profound to sort of cover it." Can you explain what you meant by profound? Because sometimes when we sin, we would always say, "I want to be so much more than what I was before." But when we try to commit, we realise that it is beyond our capacity, and end up not doing it.

A. When I say we need to do something profound, I actually mean it, because it is not enough for us to be mediocre. It is not enough for us to just do what we have done before. And it is not enough for us to just let ourselves off easy. When I say profound, I mean look at the threshold that Allah (s.w.t.) puts. A man said to his wife, "You are done. You have become like my mother. You are so old so I don't need you."

Allah (s.w.t.) said in the Qur'an, for this man to have her back as his wife, he must fast sixty days—continuously and without a break. Profound. When the Prophet (s.a.w.) heard from her, he (s.aw.) initially was dealing with it—but not with a seriousness. Then Allah (s.w.t.) interrupted him and brought down Jibril with the Qur'an:

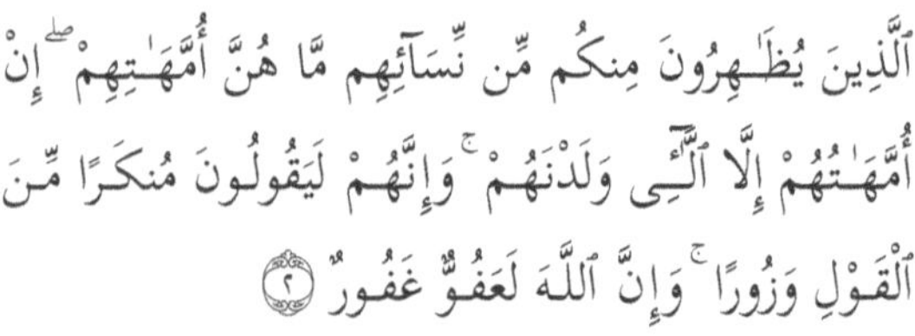

Those who pronounce ẓihar among you [to separate] from their wives—they are not [consequently] their mothers. Their mothers are none but those who gave birth to them. And indeed, they are saying an objectionable statement and a falsehood. But indeed, Allah is Pardoning and Forgiving.

(al-Mujadalah, 58:2)

After all these years, this man wants to insult his wife saying that she is like his mother. After she gave her life, her beauty, her body, her children and her attention. So he had to fast for 60 days without a break. If he cannot do that, he has to feed sixty people for a full day. Which in fact happened.

His wife was wealthier than him. *SubhanAllāh,* isn't it ironic? She said, "This husband of mine says, "I can have four women." *Wallāhi,* he cannot. He can't even fast for sixty days. So Allah revealed that he had to feed sixty people. She said, "No, not just he doesn't have strength but he's a poor man. He can't even feed himself. O' Rasulullah, I will donate." She paid for him and the Prophet (s.a.w.) paid for the rest. Look at the value of an honourable woman. **Profound**.

So when I say profound, push yourself to a way to spiritual heights. Sometimes *SubhanAllāh*, as we sit there, we attempt to bargain cheaply with Allah (s.w.t.). It is as if you want to get off easy. Abu Lubabah, he made a mistake. He spoke about something the Prophet (s.a.w.) said to people who did not need to hear it, and it exposed one of the things that were hidden by the Prophet (s.a.w.) from some of those who had aggression towards him. And when Abu Lubabah exposed that; they acted upon Abu Lubabah's advice, so they took precautions. And when the prophet (s.a.w.) said how did they know? Abu Lubabah said, "O' Prophet (s.a.w.), I made a mistake. What should I do?" The Prophet (s.a.w.) said, "I don't know, wait for the Qur'an to come." Abu Lubabah tied himself to the post of the *masjid* of the Prophet (s.a.w.), right next to the entrance of the house of 'A'ishah— there is a post. There is the post of 'A'ishah and the post of Abu Lubabah. It is called *Amudu Raḥmah*, the pillar of *rahmah*, Allah's mercy. Abu Lubabah sat in it, tied himself. He said, "I'm not going to leave the *masjid* until Allah forgives me." For three days, his wife would come and bring him food and he would just go out to cleanse himself. Then he would come back and sit. Never left the *masjid*. Waiting for the answer of Allah. **Profound**. Sometimes we need to demonstrate our genuineness to Allah (s.w.t.). Sometimes it is in our *ṣadaqah*, sometimes it is in our *ʿibadah*, sometimes we make a *nazr*. "I'm going to fast for three days or I'm going to feed 100 poor people on account of this." Sometimes it is something you have to demonstrate that you need from Allah (s.w.t.).

QUESTION 5: You mentioned Nabi Musa (a.s.) being a little upset with Nabi Adam (a.s.) because he brought us back to Earth right, when we should originally be in *Jannah*. You also mentioned that had the *shaytan* not whispered to Nabi Adam (a.s.), he would have still approached the forbidden tree. So we are saying here that there is a sort of a joint venture between our *nafs* and the whisperings of the *shaytan*—so it's not acting independently. But then again in Ramadan, we are told that the *shaytan* have been bound and chained, however, we still transgress during that holy month as well.

So would that just be our *nafs*? However, isn't the *nafs* also a *fitrah* that is born pure in obedience and submission to Allah? Where is the dichotomy?

A. Adam (a.s.) as Allah (s.w.t.) is creating him, Allah says to the angels in *Surah* al-Baqarah verse 30:

And [mention, O' Muḥammad], when your Lord said to the angels, "Indeed, I will make upon the earth a successive authority."

A new creation who will inherit the earth one after another. We are *khalifah* on this earth. I live and keep the earth clean and prepared for my children, as you do for your children and children. We are meant to look after it for future generations. The Angels, they responded:

They said, "Will You place upon it one who causes corruption therein and sheds blood, while we exalt You with praise and declare Your perfection?"

The Angels were aware that humans would cause corruption and shed blood because there were creations like humans that existed before Adam (a.s.). There was an Adam and there were things before him. The Angels have seen this, but Adam was always destined for Earth.

Adam's (a.s.) response to Musa's (a.s.) statement was very interesting. He said, "Are you angry at me? Are you debating with me something that is written for me? It is written for me that I have the capacity to make a mistake. This means that if you were in my place, you would have done the same." When you look into the life of Musa (a.s.), he was in Egypt. He (s.a.w.) saw two people arguing. What did Musa (a.s.) do? Musa (a.s.) pushed that Egyptian man and he fell and he died. Musa (a.s.) said that this is a devilish act (al-Qaṣaṣ, 28:15). So Adam (a.s.) said to Musa (a.s.), "Well, what about you? If you were in my place, there would be no different. Are you complaining about something written that we were meant to be on Earth—not written that Allah ordered me to eat from the tree, with regards to the whispering of the *shaytan* and this is an important clarification.

The hadith of the Prophet (s.a.w.)—if the narrations are authentic about the *shayatin*, it is not about all of the *shayatin*. The hadith it says that the the most aggressive *shaytan* is chained in Ramadan (Musnad Aḥmad 7857). So some of the *'ulama'* they said that it is not all of the *shayatin* in Ramadan. It is the ones that are most aggressive against the believers, not against all human beings. The second understanding is that it is only in comparison to your intention of the *shaytan* being distant from you. So if you begin Ramadan asking Allah (s.w.t.) for *hidayah*, you are asking Allah for guidance, and you are asking Allah to keep the *shayatin* away, in the month of Ramadan you have greater capacity to push them out of your life to get greater control in your *nafs* compared to when it was outside the month of Ramadan. That is the second interpretation of the *'ulama'*.

The third one is to understand that most of the errors of our life are not from the *shaytan*. The *shaytan* does not introduce new desires into our capacity. The desires that we have are within our heart, within our *nafs*, that the *shaytan* beautifies them as mentioned in Surah al-Anfal verse 48. So you know you are thinking to yourself: "Oh, I'm going to take this." But then you think, "No, no, no, no, no. Maybe there's a camera. Maybe somebody will see me." Then the *shaytan* says, "Look, there's nobody here." In your mind, you get this. "There's nobody here who's going to see." And if somebody sees you just say, "Oh, I was trying to find whose it is." So all of a sudden you don't want it but the *shaytan*—*zayyanah*, "No, no, don't worry, it's OK." He comforted and assisted you. because on the Day of Judgement Allah quotes the lecture *shaytan* shall give to the people in Hellfire. Allah says when everything has been decided for people in *Jannah* and people in Hellfire, *shaytan* will say:

"Indeed, Allah had promised you the promise of truth. And I promised you, but I betrayed you. But I had no authority over you except that I invited you, and you responded to me. So do not blame me; but blame yourselves. I cannot be called to your aid, nor can you be called to my aid. Indeed, I deny your association of me [with Allah] before. Indeed, for the wrongdoers is a painful punishment."

(Ibrahim, 14:22)

May Allah (s.w.t.) allow us to have strength against our own *nafs*.

Our *nafs* have 3 main divisions—there are more than these three.

1. *Nafs muṭmainnah*:

$$\text{يَـٰٓأَيَّتُهَا ٱلنَّفْسُ ٱلْمُطْمَئِنَّةُ}$$

[To the righteous it will be said], "O' reassured soul,"

(al-Fajr, 89:27)

A soul that is content with Allah (s.w.t.). That it is content with the difficulties Allah has set, content with the *rizq* Allah has provided, content with the gratitude it is seeking with Allah (s.w.t.).

2. *Nafs al-lawwamah*:

$$\text{وَلَآ أُقْسِمُ بِٱلنَّفْسِ ٱللَّوَّامَةِ}$$

And I swear by the reproaching soul [to the certainty of resurrection].

(al-Qiyamah, 75:2)

Self-criticising—this type of *nafs* recognises its favour but recognises its error. We commit sins then we feel guilty. We live amongst this *lawwamah*. You know how we have ups and downs in our life.

3.   *Nafs al-ammarah bil su'*:

$$\text{إِنَّ النَّفْسَ لَأَمَّارَةٌ بِالسُّوءِ}$$

Indeed, the soul is a persistent enjoiner of evil,

(Yusuf, 12:53)

A soul that inclines, is inspired, is seeking, is craving the *haram*. *Shaytan* has nothing to do with it. How do we know if the mistake that we are making is a devilish influence or our ownself? How do you know the difference between the two? It Is a simple assessment. If the thing you are doing wrong is repetitive, it is just you. Everyday you did not wake up for *Fajr*. *Iblis* is already on vacation. You are in auto-mode, *masha'Allāh*. *Shaytan* is like "Why do you need me?" He's like, "I'm learning from you." You are on auto-pilot. Then you come to open the Qur'an, then he said, "Whoa, what are you doing?" So Allah says in Surah an-Naḥl verse 98: *So when you recite the Qur'an, [first] seek refuge in Allah from Satan, the expelled [from His mercy].* When you come to read the Qur'an, ask Allah (s.w.t.) to protect. *Shaytan* will come back. "Oh man, I broke my holiday. I gotta get back. This guy is opening the Qur'an, he attends the class."

If it is a regular, it is a part of your life. You are obsessed with watching pornography, that's nothing to do with *Iblis*, that is you. *Nafs al-ammarah bil su'.* If you have a vulgar tongue that means you have grown your whole life, using filthy words. If you have no decency, no shame, that is you. It is a different case if it is opportunistic. You are driving and all of a sudden you see a bag on the side of the road. You did not plan that there is a bag on the road. You pull over and see there is money. And then you go, "Oh." Then at that moment, the *waswasa*. Do you know what the word *waswasa* means? It is the clacking of gold coins together. The *waswasa* is the sound of clickety clack of gold. You know, coin on coin, where it makes that clap. That sound of gold striking gold *waswasa ta zahab*. That is what murmurs in our hearts. Deep down, *shaytan* will all of a Sudden you whispers: "You can have more. You can get more. You can do better." So it is there. You want it. You want that but it is *yuwaswisu fi sudūrinnās;* murmuring in the hearts of man. So that is an important distinction.